AIRLINER TECH SERIES

VOLUME 7

De HAVILLAND
COMET

BY KEV DARLING

specialtypress

PUBLISHERS AND WHOLESALERS

Published by
Specialty Press Publishers and Wholesalers
11605 Kost Dam Road
North Branch, MN 55056
United States of America
(651) 583-3239

Distributed in the UK and Europe by
Airlife Publishing Ltd.
101 Longden Road
Shrewsbury
SY3 9EB
England

ISBN 1-58007-036-1

Printed in China

Title Page: *Prior to gaining its own Comet fleet Olympic Airways hired spare capacity from BAE. Preparing to depart on another European journey this Comet is taxiing past one of its greatest rivals the French built Caravelle. Of interest is that the nose and flight deck design were a straight copy of the De Havilland setup. (C P Russell Smith Collection)*
Front Cover: *This is the second Comet to have been allocated the registration G-APDJ. It was first operated by BOAC which later sold it to Dan Air in whose early finish it is seen here. (Huw Bowen Collection)*
Back Cover (Left Top): *Aircraft or speedboat,* Canopus *lands at rain-drenched Fairford. (BBA Collection)*
Back Cover (Right Top): *Gearing systems were applied to the Comet's flight control surfaces to reduce the risk of overstressing the airframe in the higher speed ranges. The one shown is for the elevator. (Capt. Peter Duffey via Chris Duffey)*
Back Cover (Right Lower): *On today's modern jets, airliner passengers are encouraged to place their possessions in the bins over their heads. In the Comet cabin these were parcel shelves. Of note are the cabin dividers. (Marc Schaeffer)*

TABLE OF CONTENTS

DE HAVILLAND COMET

INTRODUCTION

AND ACKNOWLEDGEMENTS

The De Havilland Comet is a unique airliner that has forever carved out a place in the annals of aviation history. A bold statement for sure, although it is one that its aficionados would agree with. The author in fact can only think of one other aircraft that has had such an effect on civil air travel and that is the Concorde.

From its inception the Comet was a blend of the old and the new, the safe and the innovative. However, it was born with one inherent flaw that was to mar its earliest years. As De Havilland was reaching to the future a design miscalculation was appearing in the structure of the fuselage. This was to lead inevitably to the destruction of some of the early Mk.1s with tragic loss of life. Such was the reaction worldwide to these tragedies that the Comet almost disappeared forever.

It was the faith of De Havilland, and to some extent BOAC, that kept the project alive. Extensive redesign and strengthening of the fuselage coupled with the installation of Rolls-Royce Avon engines finally put the Comet back on the right track. The first exponents of this rework never entered civil airline use, being confined entirely to the military and the various test organisations in the UK. The Comet 3 was a step closer to the mark with its lengthened fuselage and other improvements. It was eventually to act as a prototype for all those aircraft that were to follow.

Representing the greater majority of the production run, the Comet 4 in its various guises was to be the success of the whole story. It was to be operated by the primary airlines of Britain plus many of those that were influenced by such choices. Thus it was possible to see working Comets appearing in many parts of the world in a range of colour schemes. The only country that really avoided the Comet's influence was the United States and its nearest neighbour, Canada, where the products of Boeing and McDonnell Douglas ruled the roost.

Eventually all good things must come to an end and so it was for the Comet. The type's last major operator and its greatest champion was Dan Air which consumed one way or another much of the Comet 4 fleet before it was finally retired.

This left only a few examples still flying in military marks with the UK's aviation test organisations. This was eventually whittled down to just one, the famous XS253 *Cano-*

Comet 4, G-APDC, is photographed at Heathrow being prepared for flight. Clustered around the aircraft are the vehicles required for support purposes. This situation still prevails today although the ground transport is more modern. (C P Russell Smith Collection)

One for the De Havilland employees as John Cunningham brings G-ALVG on a fly-by over Hatfield. At this time the aircraft had a nose probe fitted for testing purposes. (BAE Systems)

pus which soldiered on in the colours of A&AEE. Even *Canopus* had to retire, thus it was flown to Bruntingthorpe for preservation although it was kept in a taxiable condition. Things, however, are looking brighter as I write these words as talks between interested parties are in progress with a view to flying the machine once again.

The retirement of *Canopus* did not quite mark the end of the Comet story as two unsold airframes were converted by the then primary contractor, Hawker Siddeley Aviation, to act as prototypes for the new RAF MR aircraft — the Nimrod.

Occasionally known as "Norman the mighty grunter," a play on the words "Nimrod the mighty hunter," this last manifestation of the Comet has served the Royal Air Force well. So well in fact that selected MR.2s are being slowly reworked to the new MRA.4 standard for continued service well into this century.

The only clanger dropped throughout the Nimrod programme was the abortive attempt to rehash 11 spare airframes for the AEW role. This was a vain attempt to put a quart into a pint pot that was doomed to failure. After large quantities of the defence budget had been expended in an attempt to make the thing work, it was thankfully canceled and replaced by the Boeing-built AWACS.

In compiling such a work as this, the help and encouragement of others has been vital to its completion. Therefore I would like to mention Peter Russell Smith for again delving deep into his collection, Mel James for again having those photos that no one else has, and of course Jennifer Gradidge, a stalwart of aviation photography for many years, for her kind and informative help.

Others who have stepped forward include Damien Burke whose in-depth photography of the various bits of *Canopus* filled in many of the technical gaps. Also mention must be made of Chris and Peter Duffey who granted me access to early Comet documentation not freely available elsewhere. The latter is well known for his exploits in civilian aviation, which stretches from the Comet 1 to the flight deck of the Concorde.

Others deserving of thanks include Ray Deacon, John Nickolls who sent me a photo all the way from New Zealand, and of course Huw Bowen whose help and encouragement pointed me in the right direction in the hunt for those elusive facts. Finally, mention must be made of Marc Shaeffer whose Comet website on the internet is a work always in progress and the DH Comet e-group whose members' vast knowledge helped this book no end.

Although always last in any introduction, mention must be made of those who brought this work to fruition, namely Dennis R. Jenkins for another design job well done and the crew at Specialty Press for their hard work, inputs, and encouragement.

Kev Darling
South Wales, UK
April 2000

This underside view of G-AMXA reveals the slightly enlarged intakes required to provide the increased mass air flow for the Avon engines that were fitted as standard from the Comet 2 onward. After the aircraft was rejected by BOAC it was refurbished and passed to the RAF as a Comet C2. (Capt. Peter Duffey via Chris Duffey)

Taxiing to its stand at Heathrow, this Comet C2 has smaller intakes around the main engine inlets. These were for cooling purposes. (C P Russell Smith Collection)

An EAA Comet 4, VP-KPJ, is shown awaiting preparation for departure from Heathrow. Unlike the earlier Comet versions, the wheel hub covers have been deleted in this marque to improve maintenance. (C P Russell Smith Collection)

BRABAZON COMMITTEE

The De Havilland Comet story really begins in 1938 when the British Government announced sponsorship for two aircraft designs firmly targeted at the transatlantic passenger and airfreight market. Operating through the auspices of the UK's primary airline Imperial Airways, later to evolve into BOAC, the aircraft manufacturers Short Brothers and Fairey Aviation were encouraged to enter designs for tackling this prestigious route.

Producing designs designated the S.32 and F.C.1 respectively, it was obvious from the outset that the British firms were playing catch-up as they were facing potential opposition from such aircraft as the Douglas DC-3, the Boeing 247, and their respective offspring.

The eruption of war in Europe in September 1939 brought development of passenger and transport aircraft of any kind to a halt as manufacturers turned to producing the fighters and bombers required to defend the UK. This left the remaining vestiges of air transport, both military and civilian, struggling to provide services with outdated biplane airliners and adapted bombers.

The entry of an isolationist United States into the global conflict after the bombing of Pearl Harbor in 1941 was to change the face of air transport and how it was catered for immeasurably. Blessed with a massive industrial base the aircraft industry in the United States was soon gearing up to provide the armed forces with the aircraft needed to defeat the Axis forces.

More importantly, long-range transports began to appear in the shape of the Douglas DC-4 and the Lockheed 049 Constellation. Both aircraft featured tricycle undercarriages, a novelty at the time, and four powerful piston engines plus the range, eventually, to cross the Atlantic.

In 1942 such was the confidence that the tide of war would change toward the Allies' favour that thoughts were turning toward the path that commercial aviation would follow once hostilities ceased. To that end, a committee under the chairmanship of Lord Brabazon of Tara, a member of many civilian and military aviation committees, was formed on 23 December to study the various options available. It took into account current and projected developments in the aviation industry with regard to structures, systems, and powerplants.

This first Brabazon Committee, as it inevitably became known, eventually sponsored the development of a range of aircraft from various manufacturers that covered long-range airliners and smaller feeder-type airliners.

Included in this inventory was the Bristol Type 167 Brabazon (Type 1), a large behemoth far in advance of its time in many respects, although it was eventually doomed to failure due in part to its too high operating costs. Also included were the Airspeed AS 57 Ambassador (Type 2A), Vickers Type 630 Viscount (Type 2B), Avro Type 688 Tudor (Type 5), Armstrong Whitworth AW55 Apollo (Type 2B), De Havilland DH104 Dove (Type 3), Miles M60 Marathon (Type 5), and the subject of this work, the DH106 Comet from De Havilland (Type 4).

The Comet was referred to as Type No. 4 in the list of five primary aircraft tasks being examined. The initial thoughts on its development and role were first specified in a report submitted to the government

When the Brabazon Committee began its deliberations, the Douglas DC-4 was already making its appearance as the C-54 in the service of US Army Air Forces. This particular aircraft was registered to British United Airways as G-AOXK. (Jennifer M Gradidge Collection)

The Airspeed Ambassador was designated as the Type 2A by the committee and was visualised as a feeder liner. This example is G-AMAC of BEA. (Jennifer M Gradidge Collection)

The turboprop Vickers Viscount, an intermediate distance airliner, was designated as the Type 2B by the Brabazon Committee. (Jennifer M Gradidge Collection)

One of the first aircraft designs sanctioned by the Brabazon Committee was the Bristol Type 167 Brabazon. (Photo Jennifer M Gradidge Collection)

on 9 February 1943. Here it was described as a jet-propelled mail plane for the North Atlantic transport route that was capable of carrying at least one (UK) ton of cargo.

It should be noted that there was no specific mention of passengers at this time, vestiges of wartime thinking and priorities were to permeate development in many fields long after the conflict had ended. Very few firm details of performance and weights were included in this initial report. In fact, the only set parameters appeared to be those of speed, which was set at 400 mph, and the method of propulsion.

Further specifications were worked out for the Type 4 and its five companions (another had been added in the intervening time) between August 1943 and November 1945 by a second Brabazon committee, formed on 25 May 1943. The committee included members from both the aircraft manufacturing industries and the airlines as a greater majority. These deliberations finally culminated in the last of five reports that maintained the Type 4 as the only turbojet powered aircraft; the others were seen as turboprop or piston powered from the outset.

The evolution of the Type 4 specification had really begun to take shape in mid-1944. By this time the jet engine, albeit crude in this first outing, was seen as a viable

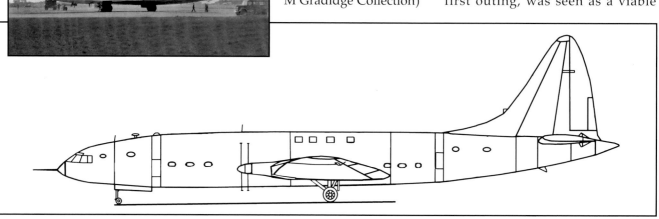

powerplant whilst the first ventures into the area of swept wing technology were being explored. Although the perceived aircraft was intended to challenge for the North Atlantic route, early studies were more cautious, concentrating mainly upon the European and Empire network that had been firmly established before the war.

The first aircraft specification tentatively put forward featured two or more turbojets of the centrifugal type that would be capable of carrying 14 passengers at 450 mph at an altitude of 30,000 ft. The given range was in the 700 to 800 mile mark whilst an all up weight of 30,000 lbs. was specified. A small payload of 3,000 lbs. was also included in the final total. Powerplants would be chosen from the two then available, namely the Whittle (later to evolve into the Derwent) and a developed version of the De Havilland engine, the Goblin, later to evolve into the more powerful Ghost.

A few months later, in November, the specification had increased the projected range to 1,000+ miles. It was also at this point that De Havilland Aircraft of Hatfield was confirmed as the builder. A further bold move saw BOAC ordering 25 of the new aircraft in order to stimulate domestic and foreign sales. Formed in November 1939 as a nationalised concern from Imperial Airways and British Airways, BOAC was seen as the primary long-range carrier.

However, the AAJC, formed as a civilian transport organisation by the rest of Britain's smaller airlines, managed to impress upon the government that another smaller concern should come into existence to cover internal and European routes. Thus once hostilities had ended BEA, another well-known Comet user, came into being albeit initially as an offspring of BOAC.

The other turboprop from the Brabazon proposals was the Armstrong Whitworth Apollo. Eventually three were ordered for MoS trials work. VX244 was the last of this order. (Jennifer M Gradidge Collection)

Avro's contribution to the Brabazon line-up was the Avro Tudor. This version, registered as G-AHNM, was the renamed Super Trader which was intended more for freight than passengers. (Jennifer M Gradidge Collection)

Designed as a feeder airliner, the Handley Page Marathon was not an outstanding success. Most of the production run ended up as Navigation Trainers with the RAF. This is one that did not, becoming G-AMGW of Derby Airways instead. (Jennifer M Gradidge Collection)

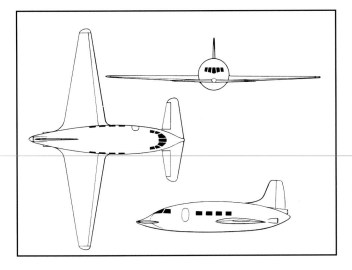

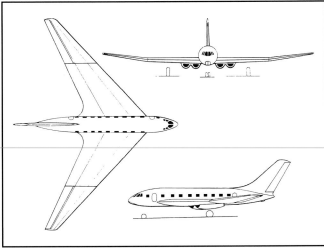

This was one of the first designs put forward for the Type 4 Brabazon proposals. The aircraft featured a canard layout with the three engines clustered in the rear fuselage. (BBA Collection)

The next point of evolution saw this creation with severely swept back wings and engines mounted partially under the wings. Note the lack of tailplane, which was to cause such instability in the DH108 Swallow. (BBA Collection)

In February 1945 De Havilland was awarded a contract under Specification S.20/44 to design and bring into service the Brabazon Committee Type 4 as the DH106.

The initial design concepts that led to the DH106 Comet were first put in place under the aegis of the Brabazon Committee. Input to the aircraft came from the MoA, later to emerge as the MoS, the relatively new state airline BOAC, and other interested parties including the RAE and A&AEE.

From these first proposals came the earliest ideas that were intended to benefit from the inclusion of jet engines into the design. The first offering by the design team led by R. E. Bishop, was revealed as a development of the Vampire twin boom fighter although this featured three Halford H2 engines at the rear of the fuselage pod fed by a similar set of intakes. On paper the aircraft, at one time named the Vampire Mail Carrier, had a span of 80 ft. and was projected as being capable of carrying

six passengers and 2,000 lbs. of cargo across the Atlantic from London to New York.

This concept was one of those put forward to fulfill an initial specification that was released by the MoA in late 1944. As this was to be a unique aircraft the specification was left open-ended to allow all forms of development to take place without restriction.

A further design put forward by De Havilland involved a tailless aircraft with the wings swept at 40 degrees with the four engines buried in the wingroots and fed by common intakes. The payload and 24 passengers were housed in a pressurised fuselage some eight ft. in diameter. In order to cross the Atlantic the passenger load would have been reduced to 18 with a stop for refueling at Gander, Newfoundland. The aircraft grossed in at 82,000 lbs. maximum takeoff weight although this would have been reduced to 75,000 lbs. if 24 passengers were to be carried over stage lengths set at 2,200 miles. As the aircraft was also intended to fly to both South Africa and Australia, total transit times would have been 15 and 24 hours respectively.

The nearest similar rival to the Comet was the French-built Caravelle with whom it shared some similarities. This particular example is preserved at the Pima Air & Space Museum near Tucson, Arizona. (BBA Collection)

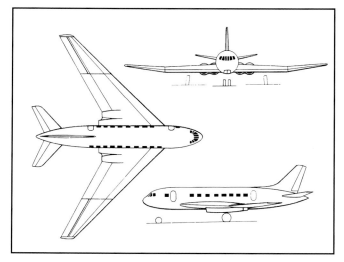

Coming close to the final design, this schematic reveals the fitment of a swept tailplane to the earlier fuselage. This feature never appeared on the DH106 although it was proposed for the unbuilt Comet V. (BBA Collection)

In order to test the proposed nosewheel steering for the Comet this unique rig was constructed. A Bedford lorry chassis was used as a basis with Mosquito main legs as outriggers. (BAE Systems)

As the Type 4 was intended as a flagship project for the UK, the MoA decided that further backup research was required to evaluate some of the ideas being put forward. As one of the ideas was for a tailless airliner, De Havilland was instructed to build a series of test vehicles to Spec.E.18/45 for further research. This was based on the Vampire fighter. Designated the DH108 Swallow, the basis of the aircraft was the fighters' fuselage, modified, and powerplant, which in the first aircraft, TG283, was the DH Goblin 2 rated at 3,000 lbs.st.

Intended for low-speed handling work, the wing (with its leading edge slots) never let it reach the speeds that were to kill the pilots of the other two machines. The first DH108 flew on 15 May 1946 with the second airframe, TG306, following in June. Intended for a far faster flight regime it was powered by a DH Goblin 3 rated at 3,300 lbs.st. Unfortunately it was to kill its pilot, Geoffrey de Havilland, when the airframe disintegrated during a high-speed run on 27 September.

A third airframe joined the pro-gramme after its maiden flight on 24 July 1947. Serialled VW120, this version of the DH108 showed some significant changes from its earlier siblings. A longer and more pointed nose cone was installed in an effort to improve longitudinal stability whilst a lower canopy was fitted in an effort to reduce drag. Extra thrust was courtesy of an uprated DH Goblin 4 rated at 3,750 lbs.st. Both the remaining aircraft were to be lost in accidents during 1950 effectively

killing off any thought of a tailless airliner. One pilot even summed all three up in one short sentence, "A killer with a nasty stall."

Although the test and evaluation systems were being put into place for the tailless programme, De Havilland and BOAC had already decided that the whole design should be dropped and replaced by something more conventional. This decision was reached since the gross weight of the projected airliner had

TG283 was the first research DH108 Swallow constructed to test the tailless aircraft theory. Based on the Vampire fighter, this aircraft featured anti-spin parachutes in pods on the wingtips. (BAE Systems)

Hatfield 1949 and the prototype Comet is seen under construction. Not long after this photograph was taken the aircraft undertook its maiden flight on 27 July 1949. (BAE Systems)

grown beyond that predicted and the technical risks could not be quantified sufficiently.

This resulted in the original tailless design growing a rear fuselage in 1945 to which was added a swept-back tailplane. The refurbished design was presented in a brochure in May 1946 to the MoS and other interested parties. By this time the aircraft weight had stabilised at 93,000 lbs. with a proposed 36 passenger loading, although further increases would happen as the design developed. The brochure was used by the MoS to issue a contract to De Havilland for two prototypes in September 1946.

One of the design precepts that had limited the original aircraft was its inability to carry a reasonable passenger load. This resulted in BOAC dropping its order from 25 to 10 aircraft. Further changes to the design saw the leading edge wingsweep reduced from 40 to 20 degrees to which was added a tailplane of a more conventional planform.

The reduction in wing sweep reduced the cruising speed from 535 mph to 505 mph with stage lengths set at a maximum of 1,500 miles, which resulted in improved operating economics and reduced technical risk. A refinement and extension to the length of the fuselage and an increase in its diameter to 9 ft. 9 in. allowed the passenger complement to increase to 32 with an increased all up weight of 100,000 lbs.

The engine chosen to power the prototypes and the first production aircraft was a development of the Halford H2 which had evolved into the DH Ghost, although the projected powerplant preferred by both BOAC and De Havilland was a Rolls-Royce axial design originally known as the AJ65. Later this engine would become better known as the Avon.

Piloted by the DH Chief Test Pilot, John Cunningham, the first Comet lifts off from the Hatfield runway. Of note in this view are the single mainwheels that were later replaced by four-wheel bogies on the production aircraft. (BAE Systems)

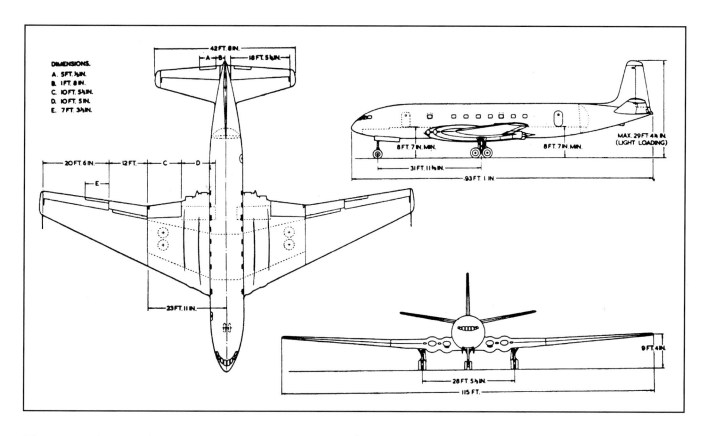

DIMENSIONS.
A. 5FT. ½IN.
B. 1FT. 8IN.
C. 10FT. 5½IN.
D. 10FT. 5IN.
E. 7FT. 3½IN.

Three-view schematic of the Comet. (Capt. Peter Duffey via Chris Duffey)

By 21 January 1947, the MoS issued the company with an instruction to proceed with the construction of eight DH106 transports for BOAC which was the first order in the world for a jet transport each costing approximately £250,000 each. A further order was forthcoming from BSAA for six aircraft, by now named the Comet, although the final total for both airlines was reduced to nine when BSAA merged with BOAC. Although De Havilland sold the original aircraft for a fixed price contract, the company was prepared to take a reasonable loss in the face of future orders.

With the design of the Comet frozen, the construction of the prototypes could begin. To clear certain systems and components for use in the new airliner, a small fleet of test aircraft was employed. To flight test the powered flight controls a DH Hornet fighter, a Mosquito development, and one of the DH108 Swal-lows were converted for evaluation purposes. To test the proposed Comet nose for visibility and performance in rain, a complete section was bolted onto the front of a Horsa glider.

Even more jury-rigged was a test rig designed to emulate the Comet's nosewheel steering and how it would handle from a pilot's point of view. First runs of the DH Ghost engine were undertaken beginning on 2 September 1945. Flight testing began on 24 July 1947 using a pair of converted Lancastri-

On tow toward the Hatfield runway is this aircraft procession. The primary airframe is the Comet prototype which is being proceeded by the chase aircraft. These are a DH Venom night fighter and in front a Canberra bomber. (Jennifer M Gradidge Collection)

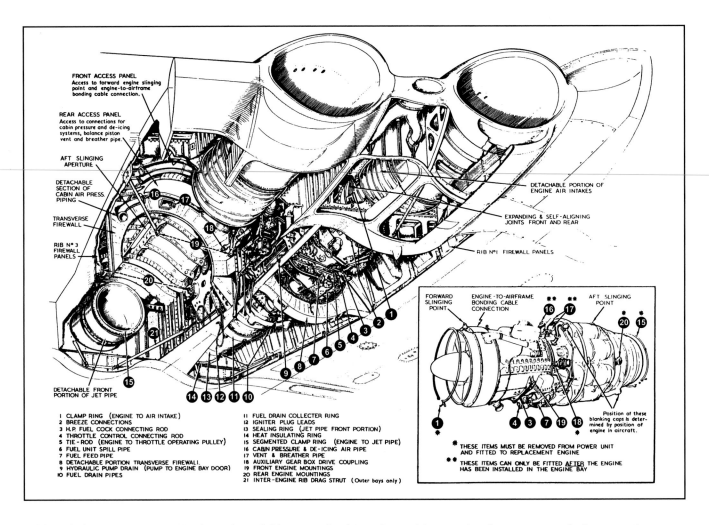

FRONT ACCESS PANEL
Access to forward engine slinging point and engine-to-airframe bonding cable connection.

REAR ACCESS PANEL
Access to connections for cabin pressure and de-icing systems, balance piston vent and breather pipe.

AFT SLINGING APERTURE

DETACHABLE SECTION OF CABIN AIR PRESS. PIPING

TRANSVERSE FIREWALL

RIB N° 3 FIREWALL PANELS

DETACHABLE FRONT PORTION OF JET PIPE

DETACHABLE PORTION OF ENGINE AIR INTAKES

EXPANDING & SELF-ALIGNING JOINTS FRONT AND REAR

RIB N°1 FIREWALL PANELS

FORWARD SLINGING POINT

ENGINE-TO-AIRFRAME BONDING CABLE CONNECTION

AFT SLINGING POINT

Position of these blanking caps is determined by position of engine in aircraft.

* THESE ITEMS MUST BE REMOVED FROM POWER UNIT AND FITTED TO REPLACEMENT ENGINE

** THESE ITEMS CAN ONLY BE FITTED AFTER THE ENGINE HAS BEEN INSTALLED IN THE ENGINE BAY

1 CLAMP RING (ENGINE TO AIR INTAKE)
2 BREEZE CONNECTIONS
3 H.P. FUEL COCK CONNECTING ROD
4 THROTTLE CONTROL CONNECTING ROD
5 TIE-ROD (ENGINE TO THROTTLE OPERATING PULLEY)
6 FUEL UNIT SPILL PIPE
7 FUEL FEED PIPE
8 DETACHABLE PORTION TRANSVERSE FIREWALL.
9 HYDRAULIC PUMP DRAIN (PUMP TO ENGINE BAY DOOR)
10 FUEL DRAIN PIPES
11 FUEL DRAIN COLLECTER RING
12 IGNITER PLUG LEADS
13 SEALING RING (JET PIPE FRONT PORTION)
14 HEAT INSULATING RING
15 SEGMENTED CLAMP RING (ENGINE TO JET PIPE)
16 CABIN PRESSURE & DE-ICING AIR PIPE
17 VENT & BREATHER PIPE
18 AUXILIARY GEAR BOX DRIVE COUPLING
19 FRONT ENGINE MOUNTINGS
20 REAR ENGINE MOUNTINGS
21 INTER-ENGINE RIB DRAG STRUT (Outer bays only)

Although there were cut-outs in the main and false spars for the engine and its associated components, the lower sections were made removable for ECU replacement. (Capt. Peter Duffey via Chris Duffey)

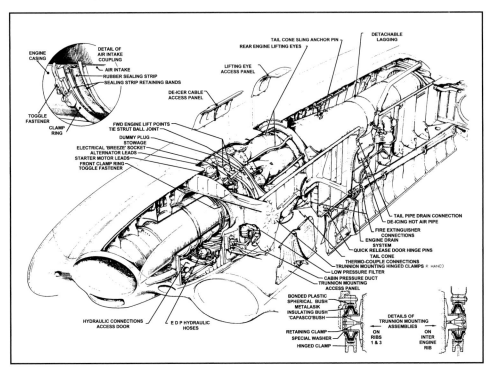

ENGINE CASING

DETAIL OF AIR INTAKE COUPLING

AIR INTAKE
RUBBER SEALING STRIP
SEALING STRIP RETAINING BANDS

TOGGLE FASTENER

CLAMP RING

DE-ICER CABLE ACCESS PANEL

FWD ENGINE LIFT POINTS
TIE STRUT BALL JOINT
DUMMY PLUG STOWAGE
ELECTRICAL 'BREEZE' SOCKET
ALTERNATOR LEADS
STARTER MOTOR LEADS
FRONT CLAMP RING
TOGGLE FASTENER

TAIL CONE SLING ANCHOR PIN
REAR ENGINE LIFTING EYES

DETACHABLE LAGGING

LIFTING EYE ACCESS PANEL

TAIL PIPE DRAIN CONNECTION
DE-ICING HOT AIR PIPE
FIRE EXTINGUISHER CONNECTIONS
ENGINE DRAIN SYSTEM
QUICK RELEASE DOOR HINGE PINS
TAIL CONE
THERMO-COUPLE CONNECTIONS
TRUNNION MOUNTING HINGED CLAMPS (R. HAND)
CABIN PRESSURE DUCT
LOW PRESSURE FILTER
TRUNNION MOUNTING ACCESS PANEL

HYDRAULIC CONNECTIONS ACCESS DOOR

E D P HYDRAULIC HOSES

BONDED PLASTIC SPHERICAL BUSH
METALASIK INSULATING BUSH
'CAPASCO' BUSH
RETAINING CLAMP
SPECIAL WASHER
HINGED CLAMP

DETAILS OF TRUNNION MOUNTING ASSEMBLIES
ON RIBS 1 & 3
ON INTER ENGINE RIB

The Ghost engines fitted to the Comet 1 and 1A aircraft were well served by access panels. Various discreet takeoffs drove generators and hydraulic pumps whilst tappings from various parts of the engine provided cabin conditioning and de-icing. (BAE Systems)

Comet 1, G-ALYT, is pictured here on an early pre-delivery flight. It was delivered to BOAC on 6 March 1952. Complete with square windows and suppressed ADF aerials it was later handed over to Farnborough for structural testing after the fleet was grounded. (BAE Systems)

ans, VM703 and VM749. For flight trials the original Merlin engines in the number one and four positions were replaced by Ghost centrifugal jet engines. Later a modified Vampire fighter, TG278, with extended wingtips was used to take the engine to 50,000 ft. for high-altitude testing. The various flight trials continued until mid-1948 by which time the official name of "Comet" had been adopted for the new aircraft.

In line with many other projects undertaken at the time, De Havilland was eschewing publicity about the DH106 project, although it was a great step forward technically. The aircraft's design cruise height was set at 40,000 ft. with a cabin pressure differential of 8.25 psi. To ensure further passenger comfort, cabin conditioning, heating, and ventilation systems were developed.

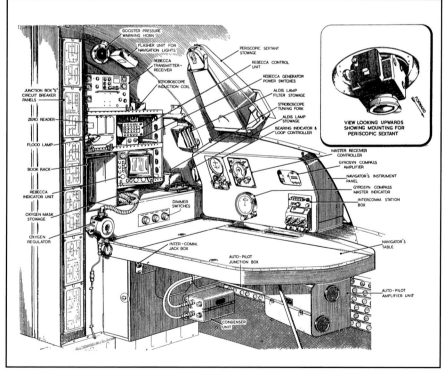

The navigator's station on the Comet looks quite antiquated compared with the INS platforms in today's aircraft. (BAE Systems)

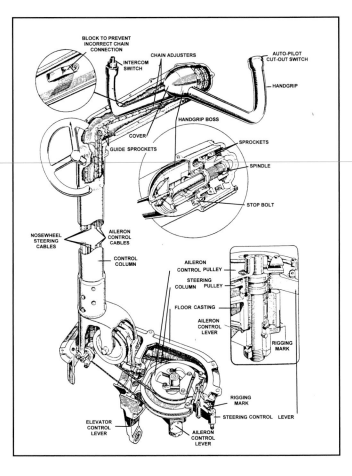

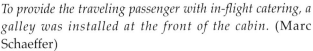
To provide the traveling passenger with in-flight catering, a galley was installed at the front of the cabin. (Marc Schaeffer)

The one item that remained basically unchanged throughout the life of the Comet and the later Nimrod was the control yoke. However, some cosmetic changes were wrought by the addition of extra buttons. (BAE Systems)

Due to the theorised increase in fuel consumption, the designers were forced to find unusual ways to increase the aircraft's available fuel load. To achieve this, integral fuel tanks were specified for the wings. This in turn meant that the use of a fairly new method of construction was needed to retain structural strength, but a reduction in weight was also required. This led to the use of Redux bonding throughout the aircraft's structure and a reduced need for riveted construction and attendant weight. Another change to the fuel system was the inclusion of single-point pressure refueling which enabled a quicker ground turnaround time.

The engine installation allowed the use of shorter, and therefore lighter, undercarriage units. The original main gear units were fitted with single main wheels, but these were later replaced with a bogie, which had four main wheels to spread the load and reduce the pavement footprint. In both cases the main gear was housed in a bay that was only revealed when a large "D" door swung open to allow the gear to enter and exit. The twin nosewheels retracted aft into their own bay in the nose.

The wing was of fairly normal construction being based about primary fore and aft spars which had cut-outs for the engines, intakes, and exhausts with a thickness/chord ratio of 11 percent. Flight controls for all primary surfaces were of the powered servodyne variety and were supported by two primary hydraulic systems backed up by a secondary flight control system and an emergency system intended for undercarriage extension. These were colour-coded green and blue for the primaries and yellow for the flight control backup, with the emergency system being identified by the colour red. The yellow, red, and green systems were switchable between each other with the blue system remaining a separate entity.

A hand pump was also built in mainly to replenish the other systems in flight although its other role was that of the last available means of lowering the undercarriage. As

much of the hydraulic equipment was gathered in one fuselage bay, a problem with overheating occurred. This had a tendency to cause the three main systems to vent overboard thus requiring topping up during the flight.

One of the first reported indications that the system reservoirs were becoming low was the failure of the hydraulically-driven windscreen wipers. Other systems hydraulically powered were the flaps, those under the exhausts being of the split variety whilst those outboard were of plain construction and section. Also mounted onto the wing were upper surface spoilers which were integrated with the selected flap position for landing.

Cabin conditioning and wing and fuselage anti-icing were courtesy of tappings derived from different points on the Ghost engines. Theoretically, each engine was capable of providing sufficient airflow to cover all services.

As the Comet was entering a new flight regime for passenger aircraft of this kind, extensive testing

The accommodations for the cabin crew aboard the Comet 1 and 2 were really quite primitive to modern eyes. (Marc Schaeffer)

was deemed a priority requirement. In the light of subsequent events, it is surprising that the tests did not reveal any trace of the impending disaster that would overtake the Comet. Some skin metalworkers, however, did express concern at the time about the problems encountered with forming the skins onto

the fuselage using the alloys selected — DTD.546 and 746.

Even so, the selected structures were pressure-tested to 20.5 psi, approximately two and a half times working load. This stress loading was also applied to the aircraft's doors and hatches, which were designed for inward opening thus improving the

One of the aircraft lost to crashes was Comet 1 G-ALYV which met its fate at Karachi on 2 May 1953. Prominent in this view are the suppressed aerials let into the nosewheel doors and the square cabin windows that caused so much trouble. (BAE Systems)

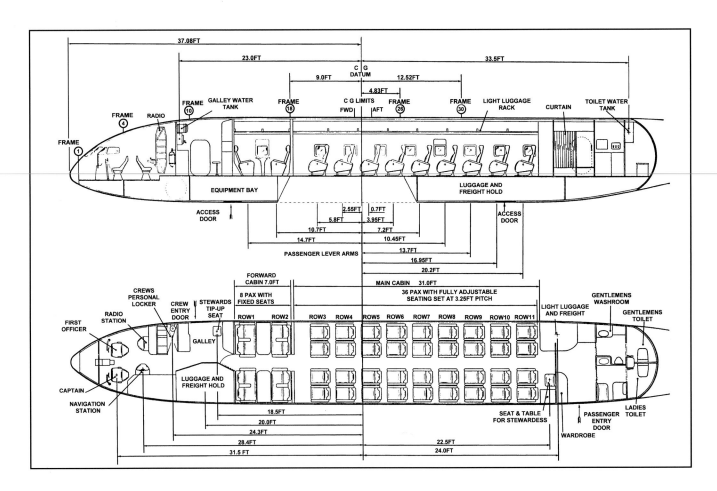

This floor plan is that of the BOAC configuration adopted for the first aircraft in that airline's service. In line with modern practises the cabin could be re-laid to accommodate a customer's specific needs. (BAE Systems)

safety factor. The aircraft's windows and surrounding structure were also subjected to extreme testing, up to a load of 10 times the expected in-service load factor.

Under the loading applied to the test fuselage, it eventually failed. No discernible cause was immediately apparent therefore another method of testing was required. This involved using a water tank which allowed pressures to be built up to failure levels without reducing safety. This method slowed down the disintegration process thus allowing the failure point to be traced.

Another area of performance placed under scrutiny was the effect that low temperature had on materials at high altitude. To test the Comet fuselage thoroughly, a compression chamber big enough to take the com-plete pressure cabin was built. The range of temperatures experienced a peak, or more accurately a trough, at -70 degrees at 70,000 ft.

Internal design led to the adoption of pairs of seats on each side of a central gangway which gave a typical layout of 36 passenger seats. This layout allowed for eight seats in a smoking room in the forward cabin with 28 in the main cabin. Passenger comfort was further extended by the installation of a galley in the forward section with toilets and washrooms to the rear. Passenger access was via an entrance door at the rear of the passenger cabin on the left-hand side.

Crew accommodation consisted of positions for a Captain and First Officer, a Flight Engineer, and Navigator. To enable crews to convert easily to the new Comet, the flight control panel was based on the Lockheed Constellation which was already in use with BOAC. A similar layout was adopted for the Comet's nearest European rival — the French-built Caravelle.

The first prototype Comet, built by the experimental department, was rolled out at Hatfield in mid-1949 and was subjected to ground handling and some tentative hops down the runway. By 25 July the ground tests had been completed and therefore the first aircraft, registered G-5-1, later changed to G-ALVG, was prepared for its first flight. After preflight checks, the aircraft undertook its maiden flight on 27 July. The second prototype, built by the production department and registered G-ALZK, undertook its first flight on 27 July 1950.

Upon rollout it was obvious that some changes had been wrought upon the aircraft to improve handling and performance. The original planned wingspan was increased to 115 ft. which allowed the gross weight to increase to 105,000 lbs., which later grew to 107,000 lbs. The fuselage length was set at 93 ft. The whole ensemble was powered by four DH Ghost 50 Mk.1 centrifugal turbojets rated at 5,050 lbs.st. Fuel system capacity in the prototypes was 5,976 Imperial gallons (47,808 lbs.) of which 5,940 gallons (47,520 lbs.) were usable.

Flight testing proceeded smoothly with over 200 hours being flown in the first five months. This had increased to 324 flying hours after 11 months. The average flight time of the aircraft per month was averaging out at approximately one hour per day. When the existence of the Comet was finally revealed, it was not long before it was shown to the public at the SBAC Farnborough Show in September 1949. In order to evaluate the Comet's hot and high performance, the aircraft was flown overseas on 25 October to Castel Benito.

One item that was not available for testing was the Sprite-assisted takeoff system. The rocket packs for this system were mounted to structurally-enhanced fairings located between the engine bays and were intended to overcome any lack of performance due to loss of engine thrust or throttle response. Trials of the rocket system in fact did not begin until May 1951. Further trials were conducted during April and May 1950 at Eastleigh, Nairobi.

As no major problems had occurred whilst the Comet had been on its trials the decision was made to begin production of the definitive article, with the first aircraft, G-ALYP, being rolled out on 9 January 1951. The only major change from the two prototypes was the fitment of four-wheel bogies on the main gear in place of the single-wheel units previously fitted. This new installation had been tested on the first prototype with flight testing beginning in December 1950. Due to the different configurations of the two main gears the new units were flown in the down and locked position as altering the wings to suit had been seen as too expensive to justify.

During 1952 "LVG" was used to test-fly the drooped leading edges that had been introduced to alleviate a wing stall problem that had been encountered during the takeoff accidents at Rome and Khartoum.

As soon as production had been agreed upon for the first aircraft, development of the design inevitably began. First changes to

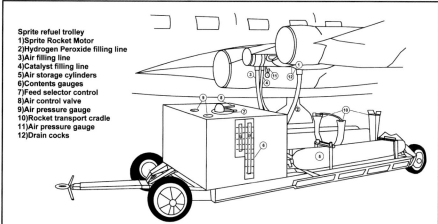

Sprite refuel trolley
1) Sprite Rocket Motor
2) Hydrogen Peroxide filling line
3) Air filling line
4) Catalyst filling line
5) Air storage cylinders
6) Contents gauges
7) Feed selector control
8) Air control valve
9) Air pressure gauge
10) Rocket transport cradle
11) Air pressure gauge
12) Drain cocks

Had the Sprite rocket motor been more than an optional extra, this trolley would have been a familiar sight on ramps throughout the world. However one of the reasons that militated against its widespread adoption was the use of hydrogen peroxide as an operating fuel catalyst. (Owen Morris)

This rear view of an early Comet's jet pipes shows quite clearly the housing for the proposed Sprite booster rocket motor. (Marc Schaeffer)

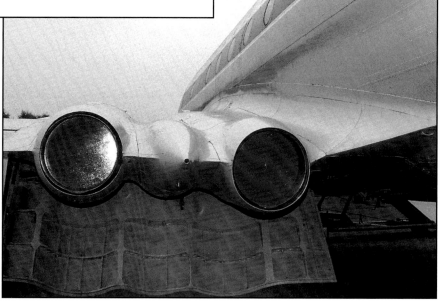

Originally CF-CUM of CPA, this aircraft was later rejected after the crash of "CUN." Refurbished and upgraded it was re-registered as a Comet 1A of BOAC as G-ANAV. The primary differences between the early Comets were that of marginal increases in fuel carried and engine thrust. (Jennifer M Gradidge Collection)

the BOAC Comet 1s were modifications to allow the gross weight to be increased to 107,000 lbs. This was to be increased even more when the upgraded Comet 1A came into service at a gross weight of 110,000 lbs. This was extended even further to 115,000 lbs. and allowed extra fuel to be carried in the wing centre section, thus increasing total fuel to 6,906 gallons. Also included in the weight gain was an increase in the number of passengers to 44.

At this time the Comet appeared to be a success, therefore orders were soon forthcoming from other airlines which included Canadian Pacific (2), UAT (3), Air France (3), and the first military operator, the RCAF. The first flight of an export aircraft for CPA, CF-CUM, was made on 11 August 1952.

From the outset the Comet 1/1A were recognised as interim aircraft, used to establish the type before the development of the axial jet-powered versions. Projected as the Comet 2, the aircraft was also to feature a slight fuselage extension to 96 ft. To allow the development of the new variant to proceed quickly the MoS ordered a version of the Comet 1, designated the 2X, with modified wings that housed the RR Avon RA9, Mk501 engines.

The maiden flight of the Comet 2X, G-AYLT, was undertaken on 16 February 1952. This development airframe was also used to test-fly the uprated Avon 502 ECUs, rated at

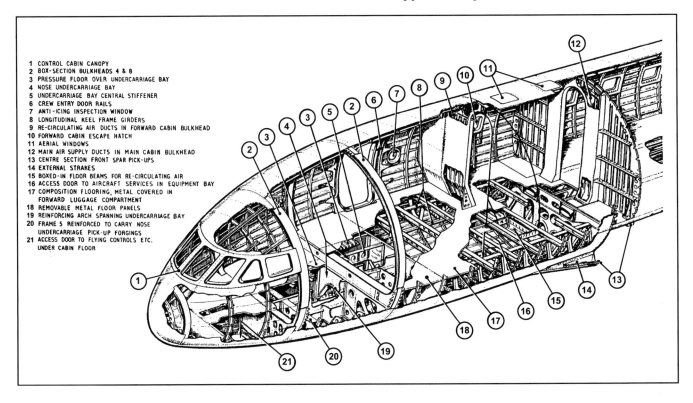

1 CONTROL CABIN CANOPY
2 BOX-SECTION BULKHEADS 4 & 8
3 PRESSURE FLOOR OVER UNDERCARRIAGE BAY
4 NOSE UNDERCARRIAGE BAY
5 UNDERCARRIAGE BAY CENTRAL STIFFENER
6 CREW ENTRY DOOR RAILS
7 ANTI-ICING INSPECTION WINDOW
8 LONGITUDINAL KEEL FRAME GIRDERS
9 RE-CIRCULATING AIR DUCTS IN FORWARD CABIN BULKHEAD
10 FORWARD CABIN ESCAPE HATCH
11 AERIAL WINDOWS
12 MAIN AIR SUPPLY DUCTS IN MAIN CABIN BULKHEAD
13 CENTRE SECTION FRONT SPAR PICK-UPS
14 EXTERNAL STRAKES
15 BOXED-IN FLOOR BEAMS FOR RE-CIRCULATING AIR
16 ACCESS DOOR TO AIRCRAFT SERVICES IN EQUIPMENT BAY
17 COMPOSITION FLOORING, METAL COVERED IN FORWARD LUGGAGE COMPARTMENT
18 REMOVABLE METAL FLOOR PANELS
19 REINFORCING ARCH SPANNING UNDERCARRIAGE BAY
20 FRAME 5 REINFORCED TO CARRY NOSE UNDERCARRIAGE PICK-UP FORGINGS
21 ACCESS DOOR TO FLYING CONTROLS ETC. UNDER CABIN FLOOR

The construction of the Comet was entirely conventional in many respects although its use of redux bonding, first pioneered by the DH104 Dove, did make it unique in its day. (BAE Systems)

6,500 lbs.st., originally intended for the production Comet 2. Eventually, however, the Comet 2 was powered by improved versions designated the Avon 503/504 and rated at 7,300 lbs. The Comet 2 also settled upon the 44-passenger layout as standard with a gross weight of 120,000 lbs.

Orders were forthcoming quite quickly from BOAC with 11 whilst British Commonwealth Pacific Airlines increased the total by six later in 1952. Such was the perceived success of the Comet that De Havilland was soon in negotiation with Short Brothers and Harland in Belfast to open another production assembly line with deliveries due to commence in 1954. Orders were sufficiently forthcoming in quantity to justify such a move with JAL (2), CPA, UAT, Air France, and Panair do Brasil extending the line.

This rosy picture was to collapse completely when disaster overtook the Comet 1.

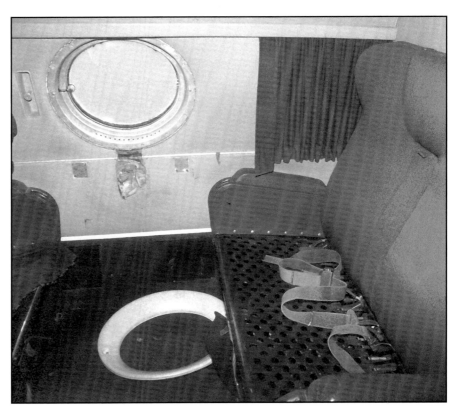

Compared with the seats fitted in passenger aircraft today these bench seats in the early versions of the Comet were more redolent of railway carriages than aircraft. The interior window trim ring has been removed and is on the floor. (Marc Schaeffer)

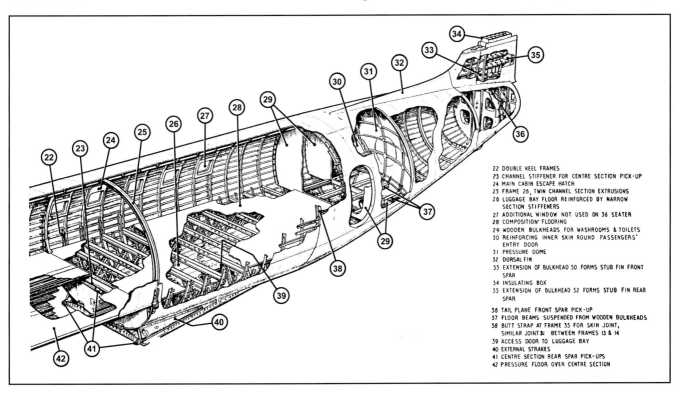

22 DOUBLE KEEL FRAMES
23 CHANNEL STIFFENER FOR CENTRE SECTION PICK-UP
24 MAIN CABIN ESCAPE HATCH
25 FRAME 26, TWIN CHANNEL SECTION EXTRUSIONS
26 LUGGAGE BAY FLOOR REINFORCED BY NARROW SECTION STIFFENERS
27 ADDITIONAL WINDOW NOT USED ON 36 SEATER
28 COMPOSITION' FLOORING
29 WOODEN BULKHEADS FOR WASHROOMS & TOILETS
30 REINFORCING INNER SKIN ROUND PASSENGERS' ENTRY DOOR
31 PRESSURE DOME
32 DORSAL FIN
33 EXTENSION OF BULKHEAD 50 FORMS STUB FIN FRONT SPAR
34 INSULATING BOX
35 EXTENSION OF BULKHEAD 52 FORMS STUB FIN REAR SPAR
36 TAIL PLANE FRONT SPAR PICK-UP
57 FLOOR BEAMS SUSPENDED FROM WOODEN BULKHEADS
58 BUTT STRAP AT FRAME 35 FOR SKIN JOINT, SIMILAR JOINT BETWEEN FRAMES 13 & 14
39 ACCESS DOOR TO LUGGAGE BAY
40 EXTERNAL STRAKES
41 CENTRE SECTION REAR SPAR PICK-UPS
42 PRESSURE FLOOR OVER CENTRE SECTION

In common with most aircraft the Comet featured greater structural strength at the mounting points for the fin, tailplane, and wing sections. It was, however, the fuselage skin that was to be the Achilles heel of the early variants. (BAE Systems)

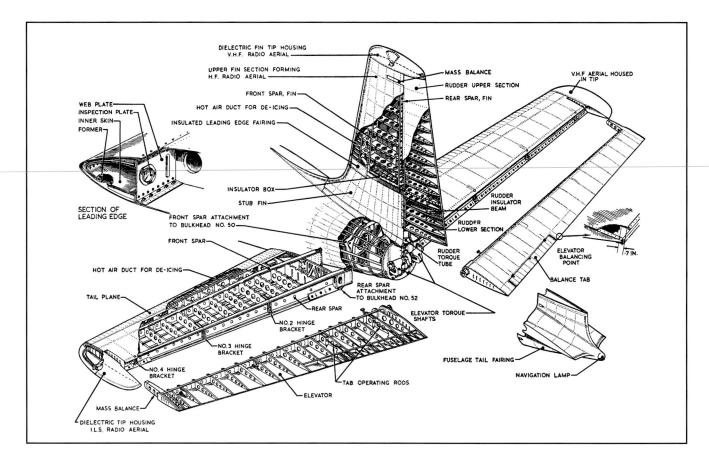

DIELECTRIC FIN TIP HOUSING
V.H.F. RADIO AERIAL

UPPER FIN SECTION FORMING
H.F. RADIO AERIAL

MASS BALANCE

RUDDER UPPER SECTION

REAR SPAR, FIN

V.H.F AERIAL HOUSED
IN TIP

FRONT SPAR, FIN

HOT AIR DUCT FOR DE-ICING

INSULATED LEADING EDGE FAIRING

WEB PLATE
INSPECTION PLATE
INNER SKIN
FORMER

SECTION OF
LEADING EDGE

INSULATOR BOX

STUB FIN

FRONT SPAR ATTACHMENT
TO BULKHEAD NO. 50

FRONT SPAR

HOT AIR DUCT FOR DE-ICING

TAIL PLANE

REAR SPAR
ATTACHMENT
TO BULKHEAD NO. 52

REAR SPAR

NO.2 HINGE
BRACKET

NO.3 HINGE
BRACKET

NO.4 HINGE
BRACKET

MASS BALANCE

DIELECTRIC TIP HOUSING
I.L.S. RADIO AERIAL

ELEVATOR

TAB OPERATING RODS

ELEVATOR TORQUE
SHAFTS

RUDDER
INSULATOR
BEAM

RUDDER
LOWER SECTION

RUDDER
TORQUE TUBE

ELEVATOR
BALANCING
POINT

BALANCE TAB

·7 IN.

FUSELAGE TAIL FAIRING

NAVIGATION LAMP

The rear end assemblies on the Comet were entirely conventional in nature. On production machines the mass balances for the flying surfaces were suppressed into the leading edge horns although the first prototype did evaluate external balance horns.
(BAE Systems)

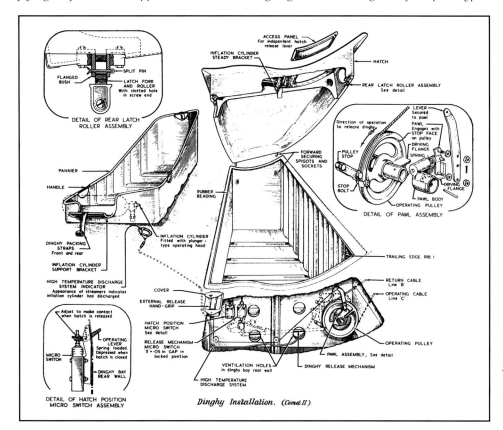

DETAIL OF REAR LATCH
ROLLER ASSEMBLY

FLANGED
BUSH

SPLIT PIN

LATCH FORK
AND ROLLER
With slotted hole
in screw end

ACCESS PANEL
For independent hatch
release lever

INFLATION CYLINDER
STEADY BRACKET

HATCH

REAR LATCH ROLLER ASSEMBLY
See detail

LEVER
Secured
to pawl

PAWL
Engages with
STOP FACE
on pulley

DIRECTION of operation
to release dinghy

DRIVING
FLANGE

SPRING

PULLEY
STOP

DRIVING
FLANGE

STOP
BOLT

PAWL BODY

OPERATING PULLEY

DETAIL OF PAWL ASSEMBLY

FORWARD
SECURING
SPIGOTS AND
SOCKETS

PANNIER

HANDLE

RUBBER
BEADING

DINGHY PACKING
STRAPS
Front and rear

INFLATION CYLINDER
SUPPORT BRACKET

HIGH TEMPERATURE DISCHARGE
SYSTEM INDICATOR
Appearance of streamers indicates
inflation cylinder has discharged

INFLATION CYLINDER
Fitted with plunger-
type operating head

TRAILING EDGE RIB 1

RETURN CABLE
Line 'B'

OPERATING CABLE
Line 'C'

COVER

EXTERNAL RELEASE
HAND-GRIP

HATCH POSITION
MICRO SWITCH
See detail

RELEASE MECHANISM
MICRO SWITCH
'X'-·OS in. GAP in
locked position

VENTILATION HOLES
in dinghy bay rear wall

OPERATING PULLEY

PAWL ASSEMBLY, See detail

DINGHY RELEASE MECHANISM

HIGH TEMPERATURE
DISCHARGE SYSTEM

Adjust to make contact
when hatch is released

OPERATING
LEVER
Spring loaded.
Depressed when
hatch is closed

MICRO
SWITCH

DINGHY BAY
REAR WALL

DETAIL OF HATCH POSITION
MICRO SWITCH ASSEMBLY

Dinghy Installation. (Comet II)

Possibly a carry over from wartime needs, the Comet featured dinghies under lightweight panels located in the wing roots. (Capt. Peter Duffey via Chris Duffey)

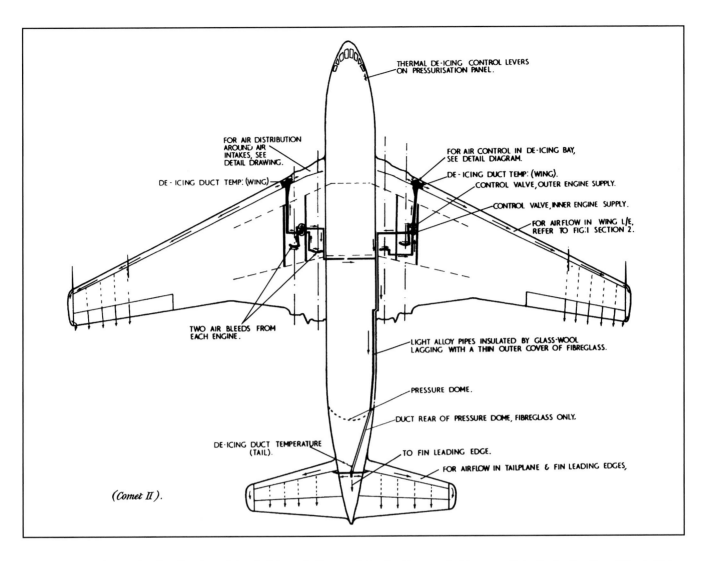

THERMAL DE-ICING CONTROL LEVERS ON PRESSURISATION PANEL.

FOR AIR DISTRIBUTION AROUND AIR INTAKES, SEE DETAIL DRAWING.

DE-ICING DUCT TEMP: (WING).

FOR AIR CONTROL IN DE-ICING BAY, SEE DETAIL DIAGRAM.

DE-ICING DUCT TEMP: (WING). CONTROL VALVE, OUTER ENGINE SUPPLY.

CONTROL VALVE, INNER ENGINE SUPPLY.

FOR AIRFLOW IN WING L/E, REFER TO FIG:1 SECTION 2.

TWO AIR BLEEDS FROM EACH ENGINE.

LIGHT ALLOY PIPES INSULATED BY GLASS-WOOL LAGGING WITH A THIN OUTER COVER OF FIBREGLASS.

PRESSURE DOME.

DUCT REAR OF PRESSURE DOME, FIBREGLASS ONLY.

DE-ICING DUCT TEMPERATURE (TAIL).

TO FIN LEADING EDGE.

FOR AIRFLOW IN TAILPLANE & FIN LEADING EDGES,

(Comet II).

This diagram shows the distribution of the de-icing air flow and the ducting needed to carry it to its destination. (Capt. Peter Duffey via Chris Duffey)

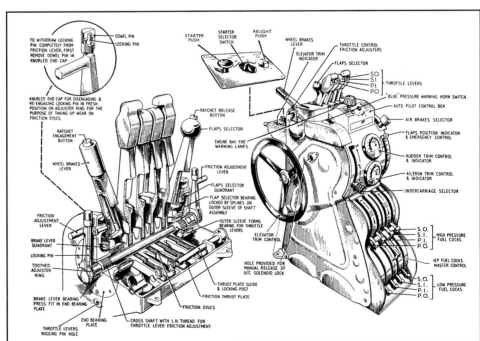

The pilot's centre pedestal contained the throttles, engine start buttons, trim wheels, and wheel brakes amongst other controls. (BAE Systems)

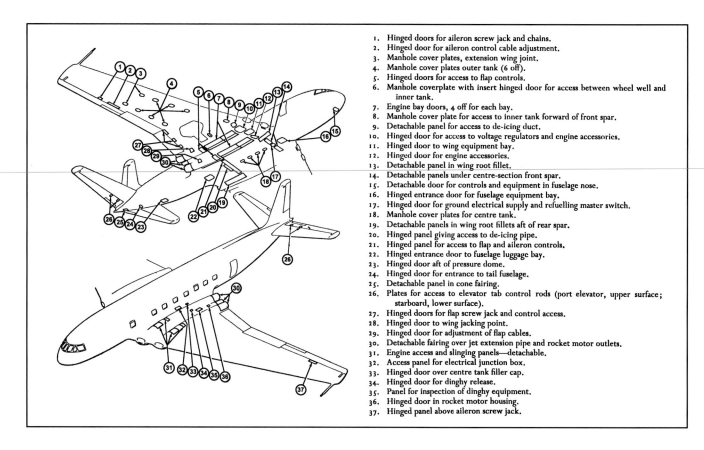

1. Hinged doors for aileron screw jack and chains.
2. Hinged door for aileron control cable adjustment.
3. Manhole cover plates, extension wing joint.
4. Manhole cover plates outer tank (6 off).
5. Hinged doors for access to flap controls.
6. Manhole coverplate with insert hinged door for access between wheel well and inner tank.
7. Engine bay doors, 4 off for each bay.
8. Manhole cover plate for access to inner tank forward of front spar.
9. Detachable panel for access to de-icing duct.
10. Hinged door for access to voltage regulators and engine accessories.
11. Hinged door to wing equipment bay.
12. Hinged door for engine accessories.
13. Detachable panel in wing root fillet.
14. Detachable panels under centre-section front spar.
15. Detachable door for controls and equipment in fuselage nose.
16. Hinged entrance door for fuselage equipment bay.
17. Hinged door for ground electrical supply and refuelling master switch.
18. Manhole cover plates for centre tank.
19. Detachable panels in wing root fillets aft of rear spar.
20. Hinged panel giving access to de-icing pipe.
21. Hinged panel for access to flap and aileron controls.
22. Hinged entrance door to fuselage luggage bay.
23. Hinged door aft of pressure dome.
24. Hinged door for entrance to tail fuselage.
25. Detachable panel in cone fairing.
26. Plates for access to elevator tab control rods (port elevator, upper surface; starboard, lower surface).
27. Hinged doors for flap screw jack and control access.
28. Hinged door to wing jacking point.
29. Hinged door for adjustment of flap cables.
30. Detachable fairing over jet extension pipe and rocket motor outlets.
31. Engine access and slinging panels—detachable.
32. Access panel for electrical junction box.
33. Hinged door over centre tank filler cap.
34. Hinged door for dinghy release.
35. Panel for inspection of dinghy equipment.
36. Hinged door in rocket motor housing.
37. Hinged panel above aileron screw jack.

Although the Comet stood at a reasonable height from the ground, most of the servicing access panels were located on the underside of the aircraft. (BAE Systems)

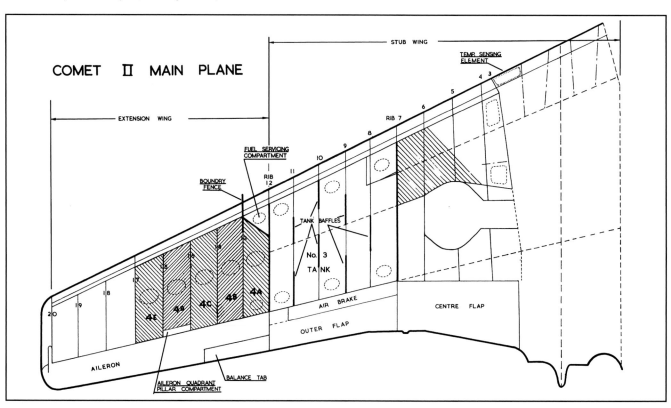

Schematic of the Comet wing shows the location of the primary components. (Capt. Peter Duffey via Chris Duffey)

DISASTER 2 STRIKES

At 1512 hours on the afternoon of 2 May 1952 Comet 1, G-ALYP, departed London Heathrow on the world's first revenue earning commercial jet-powered flight. Although subsequent events were to mar the Comet's good name, this one event changed the world of air travel forever.

On 26 October 1952, it all began to go wrong when Comet 1 G-ALYZ crashed on takeoff from Rome's Ciampino Airport. During the takeoff run the captain experienced a control shudder on rotate. The decision was taken to abandon the attempt although the following crash landing damaged the aircraft beyond repair, luckily there were no fatalities.

On 3 March 1953, one day after acceptance, another Comet was destroyed when a CPA aircraft, CF-CUN, *Empress of Hawaii*, crashed at Karachi during a delivery flight to Sydney via Honolulu. This Comet was intended to inaugurate a new service across the Pacific. However, the aircraft failed to become fully airborne on takeoff, the subsequent crash killing all onboard. As a result of this accident CPA canceled all further orders for the Comet. The second aircraft, CF-CUM, was later converted to Comet 1A standard and registered as G-ANAV for BOAC.

A further similar accident overtook a UAT machine, F-BGSC, which crashed on landing at Dakar on 25 June 1953. Although not a total write-off, the aircraft was deemed beyond economic repair and scrapped on site.

The modifications that were later carried out to the wing leading edges were intended to obviate the tight handling margins that the early Comets experienced on takeoff and landing. One of the biggest problems with the Comet was the tendency for the wing to stall on takeoff if the nose was raised sharply. Added to this was the basic feel system fitted into the flight control circuits which was dependent upon the position of the control column, not as would be the case later when "Q" feel units were installed which took their input externally from the airspeed pitot feed. Aircraft fitted with the replacement feel system were also built with the modified wing leading edges.

Although these modifications were scheduled for new build aircraft, the earlier ones were still fly-

This front-on view of CF-CUN of CPA reveals that it is undergoing pre-delivery checks. Of note are the nose door aerials suppressed into the skin, the auxiliary intakes under the inboard engines, and the covers over the nosewheel hubs that were deleted from later aircraft. Within days of this photo being taken the aircraft had crashed. (BAE Systems)

This unusual air-to-air view shows the two Comet prototypes and the first production machine in formation, all wearing BOAC colours. The leading aircraft is G-ALYP, the first Comet 1. The ADF aerials that were to cause trouble in the future are clearly visible on the cabin's upper fuselage. The second in the formation is the first prototype, which is sporting external balance weights on the rudder and elevators. To the rear of the formation is the second prototype. (BAE Systems)

ing in an as-built condition. The first incident that produced a total loss of life of crew and revenue-paying passengers occurred on 2 May 1953 when Comet 1 G-ALYV, on a flight from Singapore to London, lifted off from Dum Dum Airport on its way to Delhi. At the time there was a violent tropical storm and the Comet was noted passing through 10,000 ft. via radio contact with air traffic control. Not long afterward parts of the aircraft were seen falling from the sky. The resultant crash killed all 43 persons on board. The subsequent spread of wreckage covered some eight square miles with the engines and wings being found some four miles apart.

The initial Indian government inquiry established the cause of the crash as the failure of the port elevator spar followed by structural failure of the wings due to overstress at rib number 7. This area of the wing's structure had already come under scrutiny during fatigue testing by De Havilland and had already been modified and strengthened to alleviate localised stress point loading.

The conclusion drawn from these inquiries was that the aircraft had encountered a gusting squall of such strength that any airframe would have been in danger. Another area highlighted in the report was the simplicity of the control feel system that may have led to the pilot

over compensating, which in turn caused the elevator spar to fail under extreme load.

A further item in the report also mentioned that the throttles had been retarded to the midpoint of the quadrant indicating that the engines had been throttled back in an attempt to slow the falling Comet in its dive. The Air Accident Investigation Board from RAE Farnborough also managed to secure some of the aircraft's wreckage, however it was not enough to determine whether the Indian accident report was fully correct in its findings.

As a result of this accident the Air Registration Board recommended that De Havilland carry out more

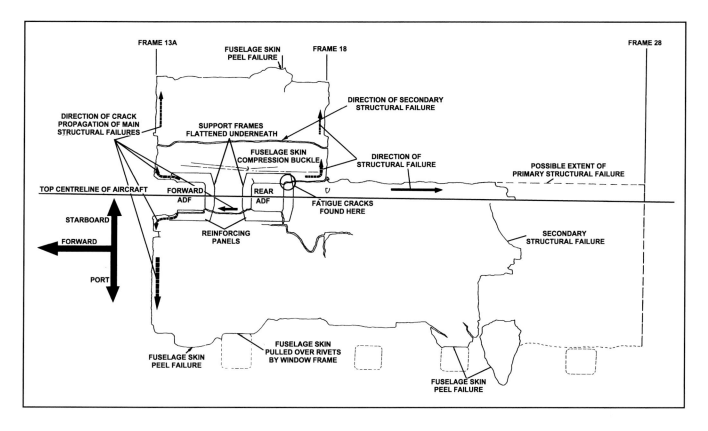

This diagram showing the structural failure of the Comet 1 fuselage was compiled using contemporary material plus data from many sources. (BBA Collection via A. Pearce)

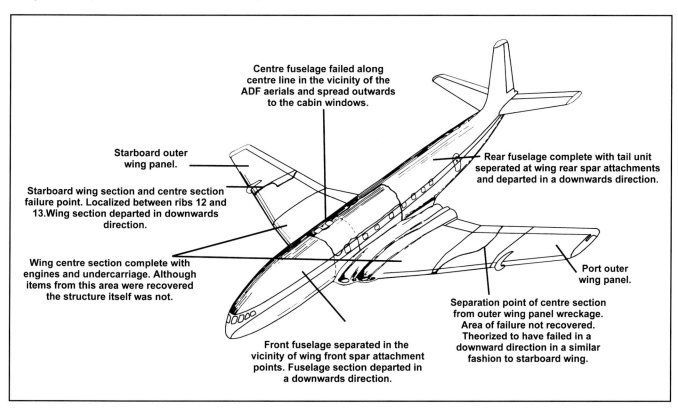

When the structural failures occurred in the Comet fuselages they followed a similar pattern of disintegration which this diagram attempts to show. (BBA Collection via A. Pearce)

This is the offending article, the suppressed ADF aerial cover as seen from inside the cabin. (Marc Schaeffer)

stringent checks upon the Comet aircraft. However, this was a case of catch up by the authorities as the company was already undertaking such tests in response to the crash.

After extensive testing that went far beyond that recommended by the ARB, these trials revealed there was a potential fatigue failure at the corner of a cabin window. The trials were eventually concluded in the Autumn of 1953. The report that was finally released stated that no further action would be required as such extremes would not be experienced in normal service.

As this was still a prestigious project for the UK the real cause of the problem, the weakness of the fuselage structure, was not addressed until much later in the aircraft's life.

Also in response to the accident, De Havilland and BOAC issued a joint statement which said that the loss of "YV" was only theorised in the accident report and that the basic design was sound. The Comets already in service then resumed normal flying.

This is an overwing exit window as fitted to the early Comets. Of note is the assembly method of the surrounding structure. (Marc Schaeffer)

Two further accidents were to befall the Comet 1 fleet before it was finally withdrawn from service. The first occurred on Sunday, 10 January 1954. BOAC aircraft, G-ALYP, en route from Singapore to London departed from Rome at 0931 hours to complete its final leg for home. Contact with the aircraft was lost as it passed the island of Elba whilst it was flying at approximately 27,000 ft. Soon after the aircraft disintegrated with the wreckage being scattered over a wide area. All 29 passengers and six crew were killed.

In response to this latest tragic

accident, BOAC voluntarily grounded its Comet fleet the next day so that extensive investigations could be carried out. The fleet was, however, legally still available for flying duties as the CofA was still in force.

As the aircraft had broken up over the sea, the RAE and the Royal Navy were having great difficulty recovering wreckage for detailed examination. Theories put forward originally included control flutter, massive hydraulic malfunction, and loss of control or catastrophic failure of the aircraft's engines.

Some evidence was soon forthcoming from the Italian pathological team which revealed that some of the aircraft's passengers had died due to severe and sudden decompression followed by a violent collision with some of the aircraft's structure in an upward direction. The conclusion was that the pressurised cabin had suffered a catastrophic decompression. This surprised all concerned as the airframe had only flown 3,681 hours since entering service.

In order to recover the remains of the Comet, a large fleet of recovery ships was assembled off Elba under the control of the Royal Navy. Over a period covering the end of February to the beginning of March, some large sections of wreckage were recovered including portions of the front and rear spars from the centre section. Two of the aircraft's engines were also recovered. Although useful, the remains were not enough to reveal the cause of the crash.

As the grounding of the Comet fleet by BOAC was voluntary, the government declined to open a public inquiry and it was left to the CAA-AIB and the MoT to investigate and report upon the possible causes. However, as no obvious fault was forthcoming the ARB (responsible for registering aircraft) and the ASB (responsible for safety proto-cols) cleared the Comets to resume flying especially as BOAC claimed that their grounding was costing them £50,000 in losses per week.

On 23 March 1954, 10 weeks after the loss of G-ALYP, service flights resumed. Twelve days later further major fuselage portions of "YP" including the flight deck, were recovered from the seabed.

The second accident occurred three days hence when Comet 1 G-ALYY, on hire to SAA, departed London for Rome en route to Johannesburg. On landing the crew discovered that bolts retaining a panel on the port wing were loose and that a fuel gauge was malfunctioning. Both these defects were rectified although the aircraft was delayed for 25 hours. On 8 April the Comet departed Rome for its destination and passed relevant radio checks. These continued until the Comet was abeam Naples at an altitude of 30,000 ft. at which point contact was lost. All on board were killed in the crash of this Comet which had flown some 2,704 hours since delivery.

In response BOAC immediately grounded the remaining aircraft. Also in response the CAA withdrew the Permit to Fly for all the extant Comets. Recovery of the wreckage would prove almost impossible due to the depth of the remains, therefore hope rested on the recovery of portions of the Elba Comet and the use of a BOAC aircraft for destructive testing. The investigation was placed under the control of Arnold Hall, FRS, who, with an RAE team, would attempt to find the cause of the crashes from any recovered wreckage.

To test the BOAC donated aircraft, G-ALYU, a water tank was con-

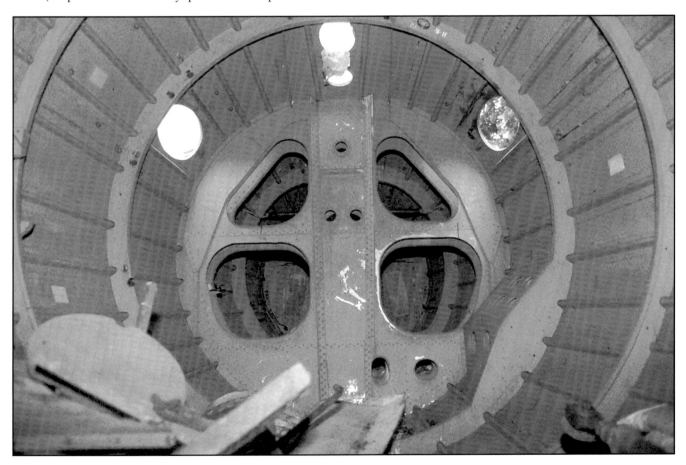

The primary frames shown in this view are the mounting points for the fin and tailplanes. (Marc Schaeffer)

structed at Farnborough which measured 112 ft. long by 20 ft. wide. Water was used to pressurise the fuselage so that simulation of flight cycles and the stresses involved could be studied safely. To simulate the loads placed upon the wings during flight, a series of hydraulic jacks was placed under the wing sections that were outside the tank. First signs of failure occurred after 150 hours of simulated flight when cracks appeared at the aft end of the undercarriage bays. Prior to the tests being stopped, at least one crack had propagated to a length of eight inches.

Even as the trials were proceeding at Farnborough a portion of the tail section belonging to "YP" was delivered at the end of May for investigation. In-depth inspection by the RAE team eventually detected paint fleck traces on the port tailplane. Analysis soon revealed that the paint trace was from the skinning on the fuselage which had been thrown backward by some great and explosive force. A further section of the

Comet lost off Elba was recovered on 3 June. This was part of the fuselage skin, the paint and scores from which were soon shown to match that on the tailplane. The evidence so far pointed to the explosive decompression of the pressurised cabin.

Further clues to a possible failure occurred at the end of June 1954 when the gauges used to monitor the internal fuselage pressure of the test specimen suddenly dropped to zero. The tank was drained and the subsequent fuselage inspection revealed a crack in the skin emanating from the corner of a passenger window.

The aircraft's structure was then repaired and the tests were resumed. After a total of 1,800 simulated test flights the gauges again dropped to zero. Yet again the tank was drained and the fuselage inspected. This revealed extensive damage on the left-hand side of the pressurised cabin above the wing that measured 8 ft. in length and some 3 ft. in width. At this point the aircraft had flown a total of 9,000 real and simu-

lated hours. Yet again signs of failure were found at the corners of the passenger windows. Although skin failure in the region of the window corners was being touted as the primary cause, further disruption was discovered in the upper fuselage skin above the centre section in the region of the cut-out for the ADF aerial. Extensive fractures in the vicinity of the rivet holes were seen as further evidence of fatigue failure.

To further extend the testing of the Comet 1 series, another aircraft, G-AMAU, was used as a flying testbed. Fully outfitted with strain gauges and recording equipment the aircraft was flown, by a volunteer crew and scientists, to high altitudes and subjected to a series of violent but controlled manoeuvres. To reduce the danger, the Comet was flown in an unpressurised condition, the crew using oxygen breathing apparatus. Over 100 flying hours were accumulated in the test series with all trials being recorded on film by a Canberra chase plane.

Air France was also an early customer for the Comet. This example, F-BGNY, was accepted in July 1953, but was later returned to De Havilland. In this view the engine doors have been dropped for access. (BAE Systems)

In late August 1954, the relevant fuselage sections of the cabin needed to prove or disprove the developing theory concerning the aircraft's loss were found on the seabed and recovered. In-depth inspection in the area of the ADF cut-out rivets revealed fine crack lines that confirmed fatigue failure of the skin. This eventually led to the skin in the vicinity of the port cabin windows being subjected to loads beyond design limits, thus failure was assured. Recalculation of the fuselage stress loads in light of this discovery revealed that the loading was as high as 70 percent of maximum instead of the original 40 or 50 percent postulated.

Having discovered enough evidence to suggest that failure of these areas of fuselage were responsible for the loss of "YP" and "YY" a court of inquiry was convened on 19 October 1954 to consider the facts. In session for five weeks the final published report confirmed the findings of RAE Farnborough. However, the report was careful not to apportion blame to any one person or company due to the pioneering nature of the Comet project.

Part of the final deduction in the report's summary revealed that the fuselage structure of the Comet 1 was in essence too weak to support the loads placed upon it. However, there are those, even today, who maintain that explosive charges had been placed in the centre sections of both aircraft so that they would be destroyed and discredit both De Havilland and the UK aircraft industry. Significantly, the centre sections of neither aircraft were ever recovered.

However, whether the cause was structural failure or a bombing conspiracy, the knowledge gained from the Comet losses formed the basis of the structural load calculations that are in use today. As for the

G-ALYP was the first production Comet 1 and was delivered to BOAC on 8 April 1952. The aircraft was to be lost in a fatal crash off Elba on 10 January 1954 after the fuselage structure failed. (Capt. Peter Duffey via Chris Duffey)

remaining BOAC Comets, they were flown home unpressurised at low level for eventual disposal. One of the Air France Comets, was also flown to the UK. This was F-BGNZ which was later converted to 1XB standard with a strengthened fuselage. Registered as G-APAS it was purchased by the MoS for trials purposes. The aircraft was later to become XM823 by which time it was being operated by DH Props for tri-

als purposes. At the end of its useful life this Comet was flown to Cosford where it is currently preserved.

The Comet production line continued for the Mk.2 although these aircraft were heavily modified for further use by the Royal Air Force. As for the production line established at Belfast, it only produced a few fuselages before being closed. All production reverted back to Hatfield and Chester.

The registration on this Comet reads "CF-SVR." This airframe was originally delivered to the RCAF as a Comet 1A. Following the crashes involving the type, it was rebuilt to 1XB standard which involved reworking the fuselage structure and installing oval windows instead of the original square items. (Capt. Peter Duffey via Chris Duffey)

Comet 1 F-BGSA was one of three aircraft delivered to the French airline UAT. The first two aircraft from this batch were returned to De Havilland when the Comet was grounded. The third aircraft, F-BGSC, was badly damaged in a landing accident at Dakar. (Jennifer M Gradidge Collection)

Damaged in a crash landing, G-ALYR was returned to the UK for repair. This was never completed as work ceased after the crashes overtook the Comet fleet. It was later sent in this dismantled state to Farnborough for structural testing. (Jennifer M Gradidge Collection)

When the Comets were withdrawn, G-AYLS was delivered to RAE Farnborough for systems and aerodynamic testing. With these trials complete it was left outside in all weather whilst its fate was decided. Such was its exposure to the elements that the layout of the external skinning can now be quite clearly seen. (C P Russell Smith Collection)

AIRLINER TECH
SERIES

THE COMET 3 FROM 2 TO 4

Throughout the troubles with the Comet 1, De Havilland had continued to develop the design. The first fruit of the company's labour was the appearance of airframe number six, G-ALYT, which was rebuilt as a Comet 2X from a Comet 1 to test the Rolls-Royce Avon Mk.502 ECUs. The maiden flight from Hatfield was undertaken on 16 February 1952. After initial flight testing it was passed onto BOAC for crew training. Other modifications applied to the Comet 2 were the addition of an extra 7,000 lbs. of fuel and a fuselage stretch of 3 ft. The whole fuselage structure was completely re-engineered using heavier gauge materials and oval windows. Initial orders were for two aircraft from BOAC which eventually rose to 20, all were for the 44-seat version.

G-AYLT remained in use as a testbed until withdrawn from use. On 28 May 1959 it was flown to the RAF training station at Halton by the DH chief test pilot, John Cunningham. After landing on the airfield's grass strip the airframe was handed over for instructional purposes. Two other Comets, both Mk.2s were also used in the testbed role. These were G-AMXD and "XK." Designated as Mk.2Es both were utilised as Avon trials aircraft. The inner positions had Mk.504 engines rated at 7,330 lbs.st. whilst the two outer bays were home to Avon Mk.524s rated at 10,000 lbs.st. To enable the more powerful ECUs to function efficiently, enlarged intakes were required to give the increased mass air flow.

The 23rd airframe, the first pro-duction Comet 2, was built at the De Havilland plant at Hatfield. Upon rollout it was registered as G-AMXA and made its maiden flight on 29 August 1953. Enough of the flight trials had been completed for it to be allowed to appear at that year's SBAC Show at Farnborough.

Further production of the Comet 2 was then halted whilst the Comet 1 accident investigations were underway. After the results of the report were released, the outstanding orders for the Comet 2 were canceled by their respective customers. Eventually a total of 16 aircraft were completed and supplied for mainly military use. However, they were not cleared for delivery until a test specimen had undergone the most stringent tests ever devised for a civilian aircraft which involved countless hours of rigorous tank testing.

De Havilland's continued refinements to the design culminated when the single Comet 3, G-ANLO, undertook its maiden flight powered by Avon Mk.502 ECUs on 19 July 1954. Constructed as a long-range aircraft intended for use by BOAC, it eventually became the prototype for the Comet 4 series. Initial flight trials were flown in an unpressurised state although once the aircraft's structural strength had been confirmed the system was reinstated. By this time, however, the outstanding Comet 3 orders were canceled in favour of the forthcoming series 4 aircraft.

G-ANLO was therefore used as a development aircraft by De Havilland although it lacked many of the features later applied to the Comet 4. The production aircraft were to feature extra fuel tankage which in turn increased the overall weight. The powerplants were changed to the more powerful Avon 524 series in February 1957 which could generate

G-AYLT was built as the only Comet 2X. This was basically a Comet 1 in which the original centrifugal Ghost engines had been replaced by the far more efficient axial-flow RR Avon powerplants. The aircraft is shown on loan to BOAC during the middle months of 1953. Of note are the lowered engine doors. (Capt. Peter Duffey via Chris Duffey)

Once F-BGNZ of Air France, G-APAS now sits in retirement at Cosford Aerospace Museum. In its active flying days it had been converted to 1XB standard for further usage by the MoS. (Capt. Peter Duffey via Chris Duffey)

After servicing, Comet 2 G-AMXD is rolled out of the hangar to await engine runs. This aircraft was later reworked as a Comet 2E for continued use by the RAE which used it for blind landing experiments with the BLEU at Bedford. (Capt. Peter Duffey via Chris Duffey)

Originally built for BOAC as a Comet 2 this airframe, G-AMXK, was later sold to the RAE via the MoS as XV144 for use in blind landing trials. (C P Russell Smith Collection)

an extra 500 lbs.st. each. They also had thrust reversers fitted to the outboard engines in order to shorten the landing run. The range for the Comet 4 was also increased to 3,225 miles which was an increase from the Comet 3's 2,700 miles and a marked increase on the 2,500 available for the Comet 2. Further flight trails in connection with Comet 4 development saw the outboard wing sections being replaced by the shorter span set destined for the Comet 4B.

To ensure there would be no problems with the forthcoming Comet 4, a partially completed Comet 3 fuselage and wing set were subjected to extensive testing to destruction before being scrapped. After full civil flight trials G-ANLO was purchased by the MoS in June 1961 for use by the BLEU. Based at RAE Bedford the aircraft was reserialled XP915 and was engaged in further trials for another 12 years to develop blind landing systems. Close to the end of the Comet's working life it was engaged in aircraft braking trials involving a foam-retardant

blanket sprayed upon the runway. Finally, withdrawn XP915 was transferred by road in 1973 to the factory at Woodford for further use in the Nimrod development trials.

The first Comet 4 had its maiden flight on 27 April 1958 registered as G-APDA. For the next few months the aircraft was put through extensive flight evaluation which culminated in a notable first when the aircraft was flown to Hong Kong in 18 hours and 22 minutes on 14 September. The successful completion of this flight ensured that the Comet 4 was issued a CAA Permit to Fly on 29 September 1958.

To test the engines for the Comet 4, a Comet 2E was fitted with RR Avon 524 RA29 engines with a brief to ensure that the required MTBF of 1,000 hours could be achieved. As the noise of the engines could be clearly heard in the cabin, extensive sound proofing was installed. Another innovation was the attachment of noise suppressors to the jet pipe end caps. This was a requirement for the New York end of the Heathrow-New York

route where stringent anti-noise regulations were in force.

The fuel contents in the Comet 4 reached a total of 9,600 gallons overall. On takeoff the consumption was 4,000 gallons per hour although this was short lived as cruise consumption reduced to 800 gallons per hour at 40,000 ft. A still-air range of 3,000 miles was calculated at a cruise speed of 500 mph. The aircraft's landing speed was set at 110 mph, whilst the takeoff run at sea level at maximum all up weight measured out at 2,300 yards. Normal climb-out speed was 260 kts. with flaps being retracted at 200 kts.

The cockpit layout housed two pilots who faced panels that featured full dual instrumentation except for engine and trim controls which were mounted on a central pedestal between them. Also on this pedestal was the SEP2 Autopilot plus the flap, undercarriage, and fuel cock controls. The upper roof panels above their heads contained switches for the landing lights, taxi lights, hydraulic servo power sup-

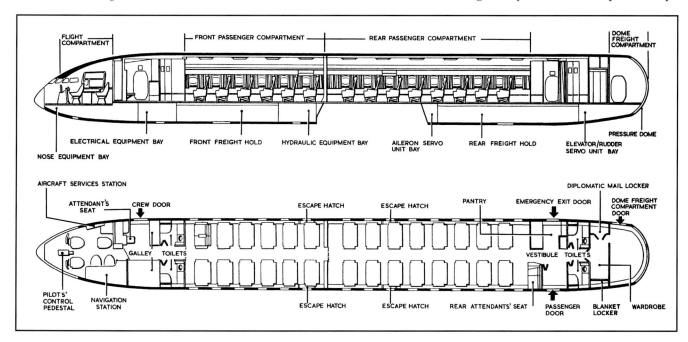

This is the basic seating layout plan produced by De Havilland. Customers could, and quite frequently did, specify their own layout. (BAE Systems)

With everything out and down Comet 2 G-AMXD is caught during the landing approach. Its period in BOAC colours was short-lived as the aircraft was returned to DH, refurbished, and sold to the RAE. (Jennifer M Gradidge Collection)

ply selectors, and fully duplicated radio selector panels. Behind the pilots were a navigator and a flight engineer who controlled the fuel system, cabin air conditioning, and on-board electrical systems.

The aircraft's electrical system received its primary power from alternators supplied by British Thompson Houston with DC power coming from rectifiers. Engine starters were supplied by ROTAX. Standby electrical power was supplied by a series of batteries whilst the fuel igniters were by Lucas.

Fitted to the Comet 4 was a nose radar unit manufactured by Ecko which not only mapped clouds, but was also capable of ground mapping and use as a search radar. For navigation purposes the aircraft was fitted with LORAN and a Marconi radio system.

The major installed hydraulic system was courtesy of Lockheed. The flight controls were operated by servodynes which were produced by the company as were the hydraulic pumps, shock absorber struts, and nosewheel steering jacks. De Havilland provided certain components such as the cold air unit with on-board controllers for many of the conditioning systems being supplied by Normalair Garrett. Other parts were supplied by Dunlop and included tyres, wheels, brake units, brake control valves, maxeret anti-skid units, and the Comet's windscreen wipers.

Emergency equipment to support the passengers in the event of a crisis included an oxygen system by Kiddle in the Comet 3 and 4, a feature that was missing from the Comet 1. In contrast, the flight crew had been so equipped since the

Viewed from a different angle the main gear "D" doors can be clearly seen. The bulge was required to cover the bogie. On the prototypes the door was much flatter. (Damien Burke/BBA Collection)

The Comet's main gears had been designed so that the rear wheel set would make contact with the ground first, with the damper above cushioning the load. (Damien Burke/BBA Collection)

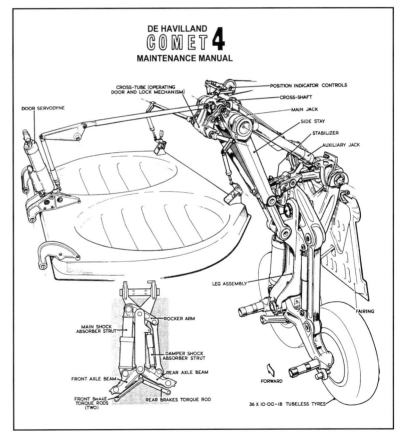

Shown from the front, the Comet's main undercarriage reveals a very squat, but solid structure. (Damien Burke/BBA Collection)

This schematic of the Comet's main gear reveals the dishing on the inner face of the "D" door and the interaction between the leg and door. (BAE Systems)

Comet had first been proposed. This system was capable of auto deployment courtesy of a cabin-mounted aneroid altitude sensor which was set for a cabin altitude of 15,000 ft.

Initially BOAC opted for a passenger cabin layout that featured 16 in deluxe or first class with 32 in the other cabin. The construction of the Comet 4 followed on from that pioneered by the earlier models; although by the time this version entered service, detail strengthening of the airframe had taken place.

The wing was constructed in sections consisting of a pair of outer wing panels bolted onto a three-part centre assembly. These featured fore and aft spars with a false spar to the rear. Further strength was given by closely spaced stringers onto which

were fastened a series of machined wing skins. Internal sealing allowed the outer wings to be used as integral fuel tanks. Redux bonding was used extensively throughout the structure. This meant that the Comet 4B fuel load was increased to 7,890 gallons whilst that of the 4/4C was increased to 8,900 gallons courtesy of the leading edge pinion tanks on the outer wings, a feature missing on the 4B.

At the wing's trailing edge were the plain flaps and ailerons, which were operated by servodynes as were the rudder and elevators, whilst the leading edges featured flaps that were designed to counteract any possible problems during the takeoff run, a fault that had afflicted earlier versions. A further

set of flaps, of the split type, were located under the jet pipe tunnel bays. For landing purposes, upper wing surface spoilers were incorporated into the system. As before there were four hydraulic systems. Two of these, green and blue, were for primary control purposes, the former being connectable with the others as was the flying control backup system, coded yellow. The final system, red, was used purely for emergency undercarriage lowering usage.

The wing centre section contained the engines plus associated peripherals. As before, the structural bones of this component consisted of two primary spars with a half spar and incorporated the engine and undercarriage bays. Cut-outs were

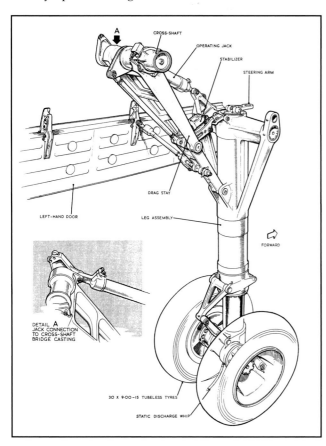

The Comet nose gear retracts aft to lie in its gear bay. One item not shown on the drawing is the spray guard quite frequently fitted to the nosewheels. (BAE Systems)

The nosewheel bay structure and nose gear was of very robust construction. The linkage for retracting the gear bay doors can be seen leading from the top of the leg to the doors. (Damien Burke/BBA Collection)

present in the spars to allow passage for the intake tunnels and the jet exhaust pipes and to provide mounting points for the engines. These were initially rated at 1,000 hours MTBF although by the time BOAC was ready to offer its remaining 18 aircraft for sale, the company had managed to extend the in-use life to 4,100 hours. In a change from the earlier Comet variants, the 3 and 4 only required tappings from two of the four engines to supply air for cabin conditioning and pressurisation.

These major after-assembly structures were attached to the aircraft's fuselage. The fuselage had an outside diameter of 10 ft. 3 in. at the widest point, internally it was 9 ft. 9 in. at the same point. The primary components in the fuselage were the frames attached to which were longerons for further strength. As before, the skins were machined and attached to the frames. Further strengthening was applied to the fuselage by the incorporation of stringers redux bonded to the skins, the rest being riveted.

All the window cut-outs in the passenger cabin were oval in shape to remove any possible problems with cracks at the corners. For the Comet 3 and 4 there were 15 windows per side whilst the longer 4B and 4C had 17 per side. The fuselage was built in four sections consisting of the nose which included the flight deck, the forward cabin, the aft cabin, and the rear fuselage to which was mounted the fin and tailplane assemblies. After the fuselage sections had been assembled on the production line the whole fuselage became a pressurised cabin which stretched from a front pressure bulkhead, upon which was mounted the radar scanner, to a rear pressure bulkhead at the rear of the passenger cabin.

Access doors to the aircraft were located fore and aft of the wing on the left-hand side and were intended primarily for crew and passenger use. The corresponding doors on the right-hand side of the fuselage were mainly used for catering crew access although they featured as emergency escape routes on the seat cards. Further escape routes were available via overwing escape points through three windows per side.

Under the fuselage floor was located a series of compartments.

Seen from the rear, the splashguards covering the nosewheels are shown. These were required to reduce the spray entering the nosewheel bay which could damage the equipment located therein. (Damien Burke / BBA Collection)

Nose-on the length of the Comet's nose landing gear leg is revealed, as is the location of the pitot heads on either side of the fuselage. (Damien Burke / BBA Collection)

The first of these was the nose undercarriage bay where the nose leg, a fairly long assembly complete with a pair of nosewheels, retracted aft to be housed under a pair of doors. Its counterparts in the wings retracted outwards to be housed under a pair of large doors which cycled through to allow the legs to retract or extend as required. During landing the aft wheels on the main bogies trailed and were the first to make contact on touchdown.

For emergency purposes the undercarriage could be lowered by gravity and the assistance of the hand pump once the locks had been released. Aft of the nosewheel bay were a series of baggage holds which straddled the wing centre section. Both featured a maximum width of 9 ft. 9 in. with a maximum length of 6 ft. 6 in. Cubic capacity for both was 333 cubic ft. There was also an upper hold by the rear pressure bulkhead which had a capacity of 104 cubic ft. Access was via an external door for loading which measured 27 in. by 48 in., and if required the crew could enter this compartment in-flight via an internal hatch.

Also located in the rear fuselage was another smaller compartment which was normally used for diplomatic baggage purposes. Fully laden, the aircraft had a maximum takeoff weight of 160,000 lbs., for landing purposes the highest weight allowable was 116,000 lbs. This then was the Comet 4.

When production finally ceased at the end of 1962, a total of 113 airframes had been constructed of which the greater majority, 67 in all, were various marques of the Comet 4.

However, this was not quite the end of the Comet development story as one more version still remained. This was the stillborn Comet V whose specifications first surfaced in July 1956. It was, however, too little too late as the Boeing 707 and Douglas DC-8 series airliners were establishing themselves as the world leaders in the airliner market place.

The design of the Comet V stayed true to its roots retaining its powerplants in the wing root engine bays albeit they had been upgraded to RR Conways. The fuselage had been stretched to accommodate some 91 passengers, the whole being finished by swept tailplanes and fin.

In the Comet 4 the engineer had responsibility for all cabin services, fuel system monitoring, and balance. He also had control of the aircraft's hydraulic systems. (Marc Schaeffer)

Over the pilots' heads were other panels that controlled various electrical services and the radio equipment. (Marc Schaeffer)

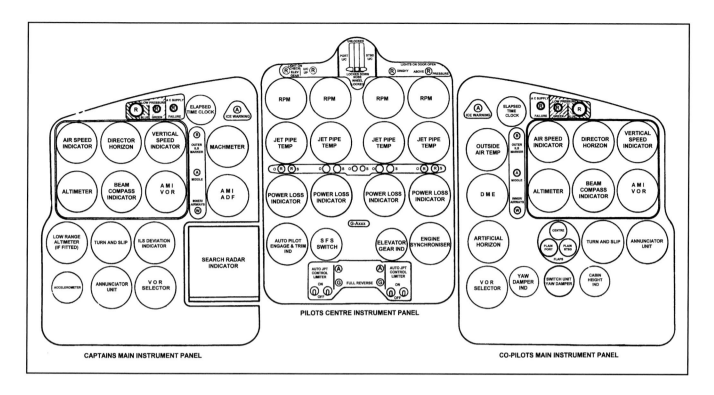

The pilots' instrument panels installed in the Comet 4 were a great advance on those originally designed for earlier marques. Improved navigation aids plus radar all had their place in this version. (BAE Systems)

When the Comet 4 series was being built the opportunity was taken to upgrade the pilots' control panels to include a radar repeater and other improvements. (Marc Schaeffer)

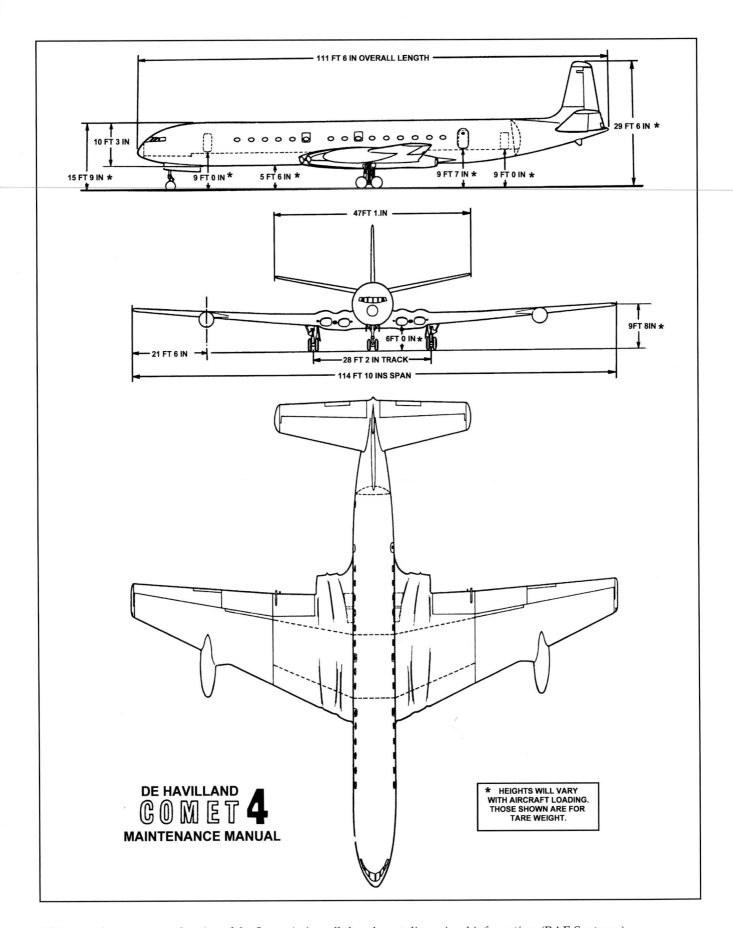

111 FT 6 IN OVERALL LENGTH

10 FT 3 IN

29 FT 6 IN *

15 FT 9 IN *

9 FT 0 IN *

5 FT 6 IN *

9 FT 7 IN *

9 FT 0 IN *

47FT 1.IN

9FT 8IN *

21 FT 6 IN

6FT 0 IN *

28 FT 2 IN TRACK

114 FT 10 INS SPAN

DE HAVILLAND
COMET 4
MAINTENANCE MANUAL

* HEIGHTS WILL VARY
WITH AIRCRAFT LOADING.
THOSE SHOWN ARE FOR
TARE WEIGHT.

This general arrangement drawing of the Comet 4 gives all the relevant dimensional information. (BAE Systems)

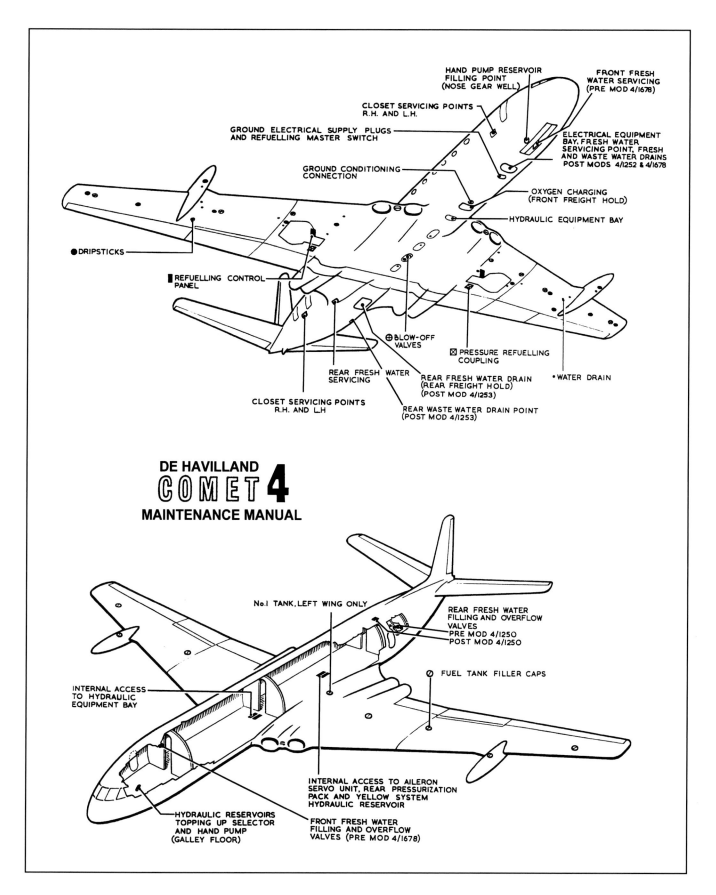

HAND PUMP RESERVOIR
FILLING POINT
(NOSE GEAR WELL)

FRONT FRESH
WATER SERVICING
(PRE MOD 4/1678)

CLOSET SERVICING POINTS
R.H. AND L.H.

GROUND ELECTRICAL SUPPLY PLUGS
AND REFUELLING MASTER SWITCH

ELECTRICAL EQUIPMENT
BAY, FRESH WATER
SERVICING POINT, FRESH
AND WASTE WATER DRAINS
POST MODS 4/1252 & 4/1678

GROUND CONDITIONING
CONNECTION

OXYGEN CHARGING
(FRONT FREIGHT HOLD)

HYDRAULIC EQUIPMENT BAY

●DRIPSTICKS

▌REFUELLING CONTROL
PANEL

⊕BLOW-OFF
VALVES

⊠ PRESSURE REFUELLING
COUPLING

REAR FRESH WATER

•WATER DRAIN

REAR FRESH WATER DRAIN
(REAR FREIGHT HOLD)
(POST MOD 4/1253)

REAR FRESH WATER
SERVICING

CLOSET SERVICING POINTS
R.H. AND L.H

REAR WASTE WATER DRAIN POINT
(POST MOD 4/1253)

DE HAVILLAND
COMET 4
MAINTENANCE MANUAL

No.1 TANK, LEFT WING ONLY

REAR FRESH WATER
FILLING AND OVERFLOW
VALVES
PRE MOD 4/1250
POST MOD 4/1250

INTERNAL ACCESS
TO HYDRAULIC
EQUIPMENT BAY

FUEL TANK FILLER CAPS

HYDRAULIC RESERVOIRS
TOPPING UP SELECTOR
AND HAND PUMP
(GALLEY FLOOR)

INTERNAL ACCESS TO AILERON
SERVO UNIT, REAR PRESSURIZATION
PACK AND YELLOW SYSTEM
HYDRAULIC RESERVOIR

FRONT FRESH WATER
FILLING AND OVERFLOW
VALVES (PRE MOD 4/1678)

In order to maintain and improve turn-around times the greater majority of access panels for servicing were located on the underneath of the aircraft. (BAE Systems)

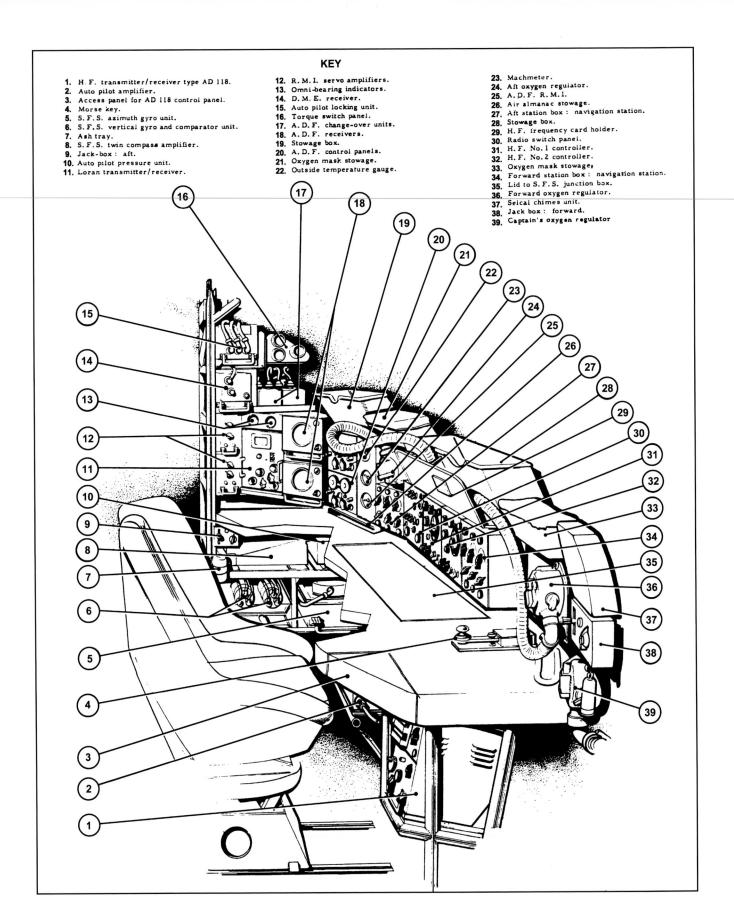

KEY

1. H. F. transmitter/receiver type AD 118.
2. Auto pilot amplifier.
3. Access panel for AD 118 control panel.
4. Morse key.
5. S. F. S. azimuth gyro unit.
6. S. F. S. vertical gyro and comparator unit.
7. Ash tray.
8. S. F. S. twin compass amplifier.
9. Jack-box : aft.
10. Auto pilot pressure unit.
11. Loran transmitter/receiver.

12. R. M. I. servo amplifiers.
13. Omni-bearing indicators.
14. D. M. E. receiver.
15. Auto pilot locking unit.
16. Torque switch panel.
17. A. D. F. change-over units.
18. A. D. F. receivers.
19. Stowage box.
20. A. D. F. control panels.
21. Oxygen mask stowage.
22. Outside temperature gauge.

23. Machmeter.
24. Aft oxygen regulator.
25. A. D. F. R. M. I.
26. Air almanac stowage.
27. Aft station box : navigation station.
28. Stowage box.
29. H. F. frequency card holder.
30. Radio switch panel.
31. H. F. No. 1 controller.
32. H. F. No. 2 controller.
33. Oxygen mask stowage.
34. Forward station box : navigation station.
35. Lid to S. F. S. junction box.
36. Forward oxygen regulator.
37. Selcal chimes unit.
38. Jack box : forward.
39. Captain's oxygen regulator

The navigator in the Comet 4 had a far more sophisticated equipment layout to command compared to his counterpart in a Comet 1. (BAE Systems)

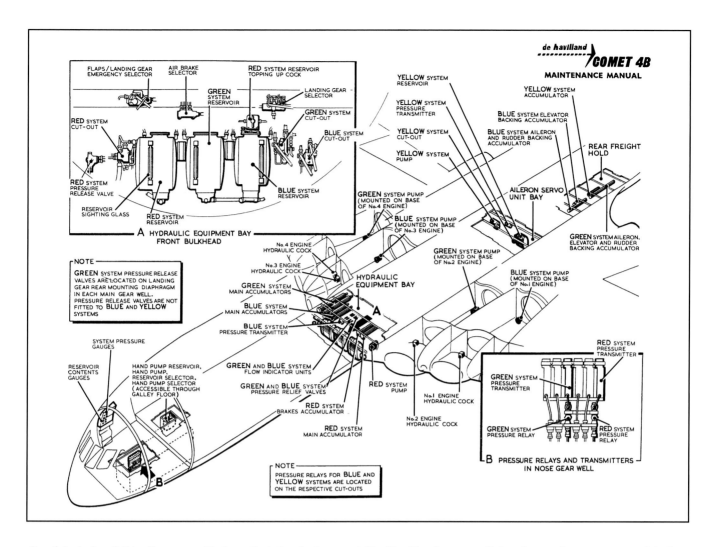

Careful study of this diagram will show that the designers at De Havilland were well in advance in some areas of design, namely that as many as possible of the aircraft hydraulic components should be within one bay. Thus only components that had to be in a different location were put there. (BAE Systems)

Even the wing pinion tanks were equipped with fuel dump pipes as this view shows. (Damien Burke/BBA Collection)

The wing trailing edge is home to the flaps, prominent upon which are the wing fuel vent/dump pipes. (Damien Burke/BBA Collection)

Moving farther back, both sets of jet pipe noise baffles are clearly shown. These were required of the Comet to comply with American noise abatement laws. (Damien Burke/BBA Collection)

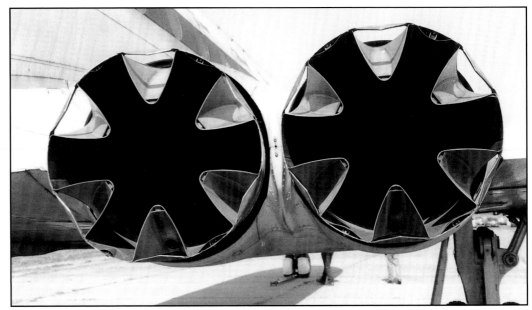

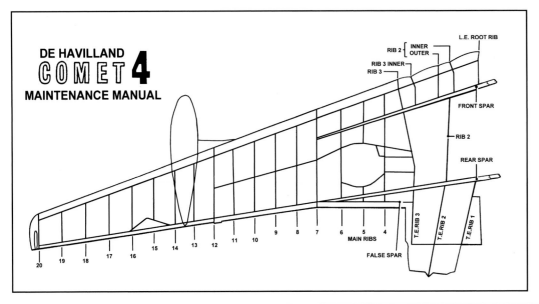

DE HAVILLAND
COMET 4
MAINTENANCE MANUAL

L.E. ROOT RIB
INNER
RIB 2
OUTER
RIB 3 INNER
RIB 3
FRONT SPAR
RIB 2
REAR SPAR
T.E.RIB 3
T.E.RIB 2
T.E.RIB 1
20 19 18 17 16 15 14 13 12 11 10 9 8 7 6 5 4
MAIN RIBS
FALSE SPAR

Although the wing structure of the Comet 4 series was based upon that developed for the prototype, changes were made to accommodate the RR Avon powerplants. This included angling the three outer ribs outward to deflect the engine thrust away from the aircraft. (BAE Systems)

AT HOME & ABROAD

In hindsight it may be fair to say that the launch of the DH Comet 1 into airline service was undertaken far too early in the aircraft's projected life. As events were to prove, more extensive testing would only have benefited De Havilland and the British airline industry in the long run. However, that was not to be and the sequence of fatal crashes due to airframe fatigue failure and problems some pilots had with the aircraft's takeoff characteristics effectively killed the early variants of Comet. Those registered to BOAC were cautiously flown home for testing, many to destruction, whilst those sold overseas were quite often cut up where they stood.

Although the first breed of Comet had suffered, De Havilland believed in the design enough to continue development. The next version, the Comet 2, was not taken up by any airline although the aircraft was now powered by RR Avon engines, had a redesigned fuselage with oval windows, and featured a modified leading edge complete with flaps to aid pilots during take-off and landing. The 16 production airframes were eventually purchased by the MoS mainly for RAF usage.

When the company decided to relaunch its airliner programme it took into consideration the advances already evidenced by Boeing with the 707 series and Douglas and the DC-8, namely that to make this mode of transport profitable increased passenger capacity was required. Thus the Comet 3 had its fuselage length increased to 115 ft., this in turn requiring an upgrading of the powerplants to the Avon 502/503 series. Only one Comet 3 was to be built and flown as orders for any others had been canceled after the accidents that had befallen the earlier aircraft. One of the major orders lost was that from Pan-Am, which had been placed in 1953, the subsequent vacancies were later filled by the emerging Boeing 707.

This aircraft, G-ANLO, was extensively test flown by De Havilland as part of the Comet 4 development programme. This latter variant of the Comet was being developed for BOAC, which was in desperate need of jet aircraft to fly its routes to such places as South Africa. The use of G-ANLO certainly hastened the issue of a Certificate of Airworthiness for the Comet 4 as well as proving a valuable tool for preliminary crew training for which it was granted BOAC colours. Upon completion of the test programme, the Comet 3 was sold to the MoS for continued development work with the RAE.

The first Comet 4, G-APDA, first flew on 27 April 1958 and was used by De Havilland and BOAC for route proving and completing the final parts of the type's certification. This was finally granted on 29 September. First deliveries to BOAC were aircraft

This pair of Comet 4s, G-APDB and "DE," are pictured at Heathrow on the occasion of the type's formal handover from DH to BOAC. Close observation of the wing root of the nearest aircraft shows the location of the dinghy under the light-coloured panels. (BAE Systems)

"DB" and "DC" which were officially handed over the next day.

On 4 October the airline flew its first commercial flight with the Comet 4 from New York to Heathrow with G-APDB, whilst coming in the other direction was "DC" which stopped to refuel at Gander en route. This was the first jet transport passenger flight across the Atlantic and placed BOAC in the history books for having beaten Pan-Am's Boeing 707 service by 22 days. Initially the service was flown weekly with plans to introduce a daily service as more aircraft became available. This was, however, delayed until 13 November due to a strike.

A total of 16 Comet 4 aircraft were delivered to BOAC with the last, G-APDT, being delivered from Chester on 19 October 1959. In-service use saw the aircraft flying the Atlantic run although they were soon replaced by the Conway powered Boeing 707 as these aircraft had a greater fuel margin. The range limitation of the Comet required that it normally stopped at Gander, Newfoundland, to refuel although at least one flight direct by G-APDH was accomplished with a helpful tailwind on 24 March 1959.

The last Comet 4 flight to New York was operated on 16 October 1960. However, this was not to be the last usage of the Comet in the North American continent as new destinations became regulars on the schedule: Montreal, started 19 December 1958; Toronto, started 1 March 1960; and Boston, started 13 June 1960.

Once the Atlantic route had become established, BOAC turned its attention to introducing the Comet to other parts of the system. The Far East was the first operations zone to be visited when G-APDC undertook a proving flight to Tokyo on 21 January 1959. This was followed by another route proving flight to Singapore using "DE" at the beginning of June.

A further service, which later became a regular, was the one-day trip to Hong Kong routed via Rangoon, Karachi, and Beirut. An extension of this route took the Comets of BOAC to Sydney, Australia, a service that began in earnest on 1 November although on this flight the stop at Rangoon was omitted.

The last primary route assigned to the Comets was that to Johannesburg which began on 2 December. With the delivery of the last Comet 4 to BOAC, the corporation felt it was time to expand its area of operations, thus an incursion into Latin America began on 25 January 1956. The major destinations on this trip were Buenos Aires and Santiago with stopovers in Madrid, Dakar, Sao Paulo, and Montevideo. In November 1960, the Comet was introduced on another service which took it into the Middle East for the first time. Destinations for this part of the network were Abadan and Doha although they were not terminations as the flight continued on to Karachi.

G-APDK is a Comet 4 on loan to Air Ceylon from BOAC. From this angle it is possible to see the reworked engine intakes required for the Avon powerplants. (Jennifer M Gradidge Collection)

Although BOAC used the Comet quite extensively over its own routes, it also leased surplus seating space to other airlines with which it had connections. One of the first was Central African Airways whose flights were flown in aircraft wholly operated by BOAC, only the titling on the tickets changed for this run from London to Rhodesia. Slightly more obvious were those aircraft leased to Air Ceylon whose titles replaced the BOAC initials on the fuselage. This service operated once a week from London to Colombo. A further lease saw surplus Comets in service with Qantus, for jet operating experience prior to the delivery of Boeing 707s. A similar usage under lease was by Air India for the Kuwait-Bombay service during the 1964 - 1965 winter season.

The use of the Comet by BOAC was, in airline terms, fairly short. The corporation had realised that the aircraft did not really have the "legs" to fly the prestigious long haul routes. Thus when the Boeing 707 and Vickers VC-10 came into service the era of the Comet began to fade. The final revenue-earning service by a BOAC Comet was flown on 22 - 24 November 1965 when G-APDE departed Auckland for Heathrow.

The superseded aircraft were not sold for reclamation, however, as there were eager buyers waiting to purchase these relatively low-time airframes. Purchasers included Dan Air, Mexicana, Malaysian Airways, AREA of Ecuador, and the Ministry of Defence. Only one basic Comet 4 remained with BOAC — later BA — this was G-APDT, which was used as a ground procedures trainer before being scrapped.

The basic Comet 4, whether ex-BOAC or new build, also found favour with many overseas airlines. Latin America featured quite heavily

Ground use air conditioning was never available on the Comet due to the lack of an APU, therefore the only option to help cool the airframe was to leave the doors open. The nearest aircraft is G-APDM of BOAC whilst next to it is an Aerolineas Argentinas example. (Jennifer M Gradidge Collection)

in the resale of ex-BOAC and new build aircraft. The greatest user was Aerolineas Argentina whose fleet eventually totaled six Comet 4s.

The first three aircraft were ordered in January 1958, but that was quickly raised to the final total a few months later. The airline had defined a requirement for jet aircraft for its primary routes from Buenos Aires to the United States and for

some destinations in Europe. The first aircraft, LV-PLM, was delivered in March 1959 with the other two from the first batch arriving in August. The second batch of three was dispatched to Argentina from March to July 1960.

The first service flown by an AA Comet was that to Santiago, Chile, which commenced in April 1960. From that point the airline extended

This very clean view of G-APDC shows an aircraft on loan to MEA from BOAC. The oval windows installed in the Comet from the Mk.2 onward are very evident. (C P Russell Smith Collection)

Comet 4B, G-APMA, was delivered to BEA on 15 April 1958. As the aircraft was required for high intensity short-haul journeys, the extra fuel capacity offered by the wing pinion tanks was not required. (BAE Systems)

its Comet usage throughout Latin America and into the United States with Miami and New York being favoured destinations. Eventually the airline reached Europe, thus it was not unusual to see an Aerolineas aircraft on the ramp at Heathrow.

Due to the nature and intensity of the airline's scheduling it is not surprising to find that some of the Comets were lost to accidents. Comet 4 LV-AHP was totally destroyed on 27 August 1959 when it hit a hill in bad weather on approach to Asuncion. In 1960 another aircraft was written off, although this time loss of life was minimal, when LV-AHO made a heavy landing at Buenos Aires on 20 February. Such was the extent of the damage that the aircraft was written off for spares recovery. The final AA

crash involved LV-AHR which hit trees on takeoff from Sao Paulo airport on 23 November 1961.

The remaining three aircraft were bolstered by the purchase of a single Comet 4C, LV-AIB, which was delivered on 27 April 1962. Due to its inherent longer range this aircraft took over some of the extended routes. Eventually the Comets were superseded by Boeing 707 aircraft, although they were to remain in the inventory flying local- and short-haul services. By 1971 the Comets had been retired and were eventually sold to Dan Air to join its ever-increasing fleet.

Two other operators in Latin America are also worthy of mention. The first is Mexicana, which purchased an ex-BOAC aircraft on 3 December 1964 as XA-NAP. This air-

craft remained in service until June 1971. Another ex-BOAC aircraft in Mexican service was XA-POW which was on long-term lease from November 1965 until December 1969. This initial experience with the first version Comet 4 was to lead on to a larger sales volume later with the longer-range variants.

Our last port of call in Latin America is to Ecuador and AREA, which purchased G-APDI from BOAC in 1965. Reregistered as HC-ALT, the Comet was flown to the Mexicana base at Mexico City for modification work. Completed by March 1966 the aircraft then entered service with the airline. Services were flown from Quito to various destinations in America including Bogota and Guayaquil in the South whilst the almost obligatory run to

Miami appeared early on in the schedule. The usage of the Comet by AREA only lasted for two years as it was withdrawn in Miami in 1968.

On the African continent, East African Airlines became a Comet customer in 1960 when it placed an order for two aircraft with De Havilland. Run as a government co-operative between Kenya, Uganda, and Tanzania the aircraft were required to compete with the jet services flown by BOAC. Ordered in 1958 both aircraft entered service during 1960 and encompassed such destinations as Nairobi, Entebbe, Dar-es-Saalam, and London in their lexicon.

So successful were the Comets that at various times at least four other aircraft were operated under lease conditions. An extension to the airline's routes took them to India and Pakistan where the destinations were Bombay and Karachi respectively. One route that disappeared in late 1963 was the twice-weekly run to Johannesburg as South Africa increased its grip on apartheid.

EAA retained the Comet in front line usage until February 1971 although by this time they were confined to secondary routes, the primaries being the purview of the Vickers Super VC-10 which was introduced in 1966.

Moving further to the east, Malaysian Airways was an early customer for the redundant BOAC Comet fleet. The airline was already quite familiar with the type, having utilised it under lease to connect to Singapore and London. During the period of leasing one aircraft, G-APDH was written off after landing when it left the runway causing extensive damage to the undercarriage and its mounts. Malaysian Airways then purchased five aircraft plus spares from BOAC. The first of these, 9M-AOB, once G-APDB, was delivered in September 1965 with the last entering service in January of the following year.

Operating routes for the newly acquired Comets initially concentrated upon flights to Europe, India, and the Gulf States. This range of opera-

The second Comet 4B delivered to BEA was G-APMB seen here on the ground at Heathrow. The location of the ground power socket under the forward fuselage is clearly visible. (C P Russell Smith Collection)

Wearing the earliest BEA markings is Comet 3, G-ANLO. Note that the outer wing panels are of the short-span type required for the BEA Comet 4B. (Jennifer M Gradidge Collection)

BEA Airtours received G-APMC from the parent company after it had been converted to cater for the high-density short-haul tourist market. (Jennifer M Gradidge Collection)

tions was soon expanded to include numerous places within Southeast Asia plus an extension to Australia.

In 1966, a consolidation of airlines in the region took place when Malaysian Airways merged with Singapore Airways to create Malaysian-Singapore Airways. As the Comets were part of a joint fleet, three were given new Singapore registrations whilst the others retained their original identities. The five aircraft continued to soldier on in service with MSA until replaced in service in 1969 by far newer products mainly from the Boeing stable.

The next variant in the Comet line came about as the result of a

All versions of the Comet 4 series were fitted with noise suppression baffles to comply with US noise level regulations. This is SX-DAK on the occasion of its transfer to Olympic Airways in 1960. (Ray Deacon)

cancellation. In July 1965 Capital Airlines placed an order with De Havilland for 14 aircraft. Four were to be the standard Comet 4 whilst the remainder were a new type, the 4A. This version was intended to have a longer fuselage with a decreased wing span. It was intended for high-density, short-haul routes. Unfortunately, financial problems forced Capital into a merger with United Airlines. The resulting airline, having no need for the Comet, canceled the order.

It was at this time that BEA was on the lookout for a jet airliner to bring the company up to the same level as its competitors within Europe. The origins of this desire stemmed from a business forecast developed in 1957, which determined that the airline should enter the jet age by 1960. It had initially pitched for the rear-engined Trident from De Havilland, although estimates by the company placed deliveries of the first examples of that aircraft in 1963 at the earliest.

BEA cast around for an interim aircraft to carry the company to the Trident introduction date. By this time the Comets for Capital had been canceled and De Havilland offered a revamped version known as the 4B to the airline. This featured a high-density layout able to accommodate over 100 passengers in tourist configuration or 87 in a more conventional first/tourist setting.

To prove the design changes the sole Comet 3, G-ANLO, was fitted with the new shorter span outer wing sections, first flying in this new guise on 21 August 1958 complete with BEA colour scheme. After flight testing, the Comet — by now redesignated 3B — was used for conversion training by BEA crews before finally retiring from civilian usage. The contract for the BEA Comets totaled six in all and was confirmed

This view of a Mexicana Comet 4C reveals the type's lineage that stretches back to the first prototype, G-ALVG. (BAE Systems)

in March 1957 for delivery in 1959.

On 27 June 1959 the first Comet 4B for BEA, G-APMA, made its maiden flight. It was quickly followed by "MB" which became the first aircraft delivered for service to BEA, the first aircraft being retained for crew conversion and other tasks. The first route proving flight was undertaken in December when aircraft "MB" flew from Heathrow to Moscow. At first BEA Comet operations were run on an ad hoc basis, aircraft being used to replace the regular performer on some routes in the event of a primary aircraft defect.

Full time regular operations began on 1 April 1960 with a scheduled run to Tel-Aviv. Using London as the prime hub, a whole network of routes was assembled including

Nicosia, Moscow, Malta, Nice, and Warsaw. Later, in competition with their European rivals, BEA began using its Comets on the Zurich route to which was added services to Copenhagen, Oslo, and Stockholm. Comet 4B, G-APMB, still exists albeit with its wings in a truncated form. It is retained at Gatwick by the BAA as a ground-handling trainer.

Such was the intensity of services provided by BEA that further aircraft were ordered. Three more were contracted for on 19 July 1960 whilst a further two were ordered on 22 December. A final contract for another two aircraft was placed on 20 January 1961. This resulted in the final Comet delivery to BEA being G-ARJN, which arrived at Heathrow on 4 August 1961.

Once the Comet had become firmly established in the BEA inventory, the chance was taken to utilise the fleet further and earn extra revenue by chartering aircraft to associate companies. Those involved included the Portuguese carrier TAP whilst round the corner, in the Mediterranean, Cyprus Airways utilised the aircraft on some of its more prestigious routes. Malta Airways in the region also benefited from its ties to BEA, using the Comet on runs to London.

For BEA, however, it was not all smooth sailing as events on 12 October 1967 were to show. Aircraft G-ARCO, en route from Cyprus to London, was blown apart by a terrorist bomb. This flight had originally been scheduled to carry the Cypriot leader Archbishop Makarios on a visit to London. At the last moment the Cypriot leader's flight was switched to another service for security reasons. All 59 passengers and seven crew were killed.

Other changes also affected the status of the BEA Comet fleet with the introduction of the DH Trident and BAC 1-11 into service. With the spare capacity now available, BEA formed a subsidiary company — BEA Airtours. This was squarely aimed at the IT end of the market. The first service operated by a rebadged Comet took place on 6 March 1970 when G-ARJL was flown to Palma. From this point the destination range grew to include Alicante, Gerona, Ibiza, Malaga, Nicosia, Palma, Pisa, Rimini, Tenerife, Trieste, and Vienna. Further work was found for the Airtours' aircraft on behalf of other IT operators including Thomas Cook and Exchange Travel. However, the Comet's days of involvement in this level of service were numbered as surplus BOAC Boeing 707s were purchased by BEA for the IT role. Not only were they faster, they could carry a greater payload over longer distances. Thus on 31 October 1973 the final IT flight by a Comet, G-ARJL, was undertaken and covered a run from Gatwick to Paris.

This demise of the Comet in Airtours' use had been preceded by that of the final aircraft retained by the parent company. Although the greater majority had moved over to the IT arm, one aircraft was retained as cover for shortages. This resulted in G-APMA flying steadily throughout 1970-71 before it made its final flight on 31 October. The withdrawal of this Comet plus its opposite number in Airtours' colours resulted in the final disappearance of the type after 12 years in frontline service. During that time over nine million

The steep nose profile of the Comet is illustrated well in this view of LV-AHN. Such a steep drop resulted in good visibility and rain dispersal characteristics. (C P Russell Smith Collection)

On its belly and fully stripped of removable components for reuse as spares, this Mexicana Comet 4C, XA-NAP, has reached the end of the road. The overwing escape points have been exercised thus revealing quite clearly their location. (Jennifer M Gradidge Collection)

people had been carried over a distance of 130 million route miles.

Only one other buyer of new build aircraft purchased the Comet 4B from De Havilland — this was the Greek airline Olympic which obtained a batch of four. The initial order was placed in July 1959 with deliveries to commence in April 1960. The first flight from Athens to London was undertaken on 18 May. Once all four were in service, plus a fifth leased from BEA, the service was expanded throughout Europe and the Middle East. After nine years of stalwart service, the Comets were retired in favour of various Boeing products.

All four of the Olympic aircraft, plus one of the retired BEA Comets, were passed onto another UK operator — Channel Airways. These five aircraft entered service in 1970 and were seen by many as the cause of the company's demise in February 1972 when it filed for bankruptcy. The purchase of the Comets had not included a significant enough spares package, thus by 1971 technical

delays had meant that IT operators were switching their business to other operators. The Comets, however, lived to fly another day as they passed onto the biggest fleet operator of the type — Dan Air.

The final Comet 4 variant, the 4C, was also the most successful in terms of general sales.

This particular build of the air-

craft featured the longer wing span inherited from the basic Comet 4 plus the increased fuel capacity and AUW from the same source. The fuselage, however, was from the 4B, which was some three feet longer. This final version was intended primarily as a long-range, long-haul machine that found greater favour in the overseas marketplace.

In order to cool the various engine zones and services, a selection of cooling intakes and exhaust vents were located in the wing top surface above the engine bays. (Jennifer M Gradidge Collection)

When this photo was taken none on board could realise that XA-NAT of Mexicana Guest would be badly damaged in a landing accident in later years. In happier times the ground crew carry out their final checks before the Comet departs. (C P Russell Smith Collection)

Comet 4C SU-ALE of United Arab Airlines is undergoing rectification after a hydraulic component change. A test rig is plugged in to the far side of the aircraft whilst one of the engine bay doors is open for functional and leak checking purposes. (C P Russell Smith Collection)

The first order for this version came from Mexicana whose initial order covered three aircraft at a cost of $14 million and was confirmed in September 1958. The first aircraft, initially registered G-AOVU, made its maiden flight on 31 October 1959. It would later be registered XA-NAR after type certification and delivery. The first Comet 4C delivered to Mexico direct was the second of the batch, XA-NAS, which arrived in January 1960. The first build aircraft finally arrived in America in June of that year.

Services covered by the Mexicana Comets included the Mexico-to-Los Angeles run which began on 4 July 1960 and marked the type's entry into commercial usage. Other destinations later added to the airline's repertoire included New York, San Antonio, San Francisco, and Chicago all of which flew under the inclusive title of "Golden Aztec."

A further option placed by Mexicana for two more aircraft was not exercised due to financial problems, although the airline did eventually lease a further two Comets from BOAC. These were G-APDT from November 1965 to December 1969 and G-APDR from December 1964, although the latter was purchased outright soon after.

Given the airline's critical financial state it soon linked up with another more profitable partner. This was Guest Aerovias Mexico whose primary trunk routes included many of the major Latin American capitals plus destinations in Europe. The operating agreement between the two airlines came into force in December 1960 to take effect from the beginning of the following year. This placed the five in-use Comets into service on the primary routes of both companies to which end some aircraft were given joint Mexicana-Guest titling.

After 10 years of sterling service, the Comet flew its final service for Mexicana-Guest in the run to San Antonio on 1 December 1970. After withdrawal the aircraft were placed in storage for possible resale. Eventually parties in the United States purchased all three.

Further overseas sales were generated in both the Middle East and North Africa, the first such purchase being made by Misrair of Egypt which was to become United Arab Airlines in December 1960. First orders placed for the Comet 4C were received in 1959 and were to eventually total nine in number. The first aircraft to be delivered, SU-ALC, arrived in Cairo on 10 June 1960. The following month saw the Comet begin route flying to Athens, London, Rome, and Beirut. A second order for a further two airframes was placed in 1961, this being followed by a third in 1962 for three more. A final Comet was ordered in 1964.

By the time the last aircraft had been delivered, the airline was flying services to destinations throughout the Middle and Far East, plus an extensive selection of services to Europe was to evolve. The Comet's grip on long haul international routes began to lessen from 1970 when Egyptair, as Misrair had

This underside view of SU-ALE reveals the jet pipe tunnels that are normally covered by the split flaps. (C P Russell Smith Collection)

become, began to substitute them with Boeing 707s. However, some of the shorter international routes remained in the aircraft's purview until they were finally withdrawn in 1976. A short period of storage for the four survivors at Cairo followed until they were sold to Dan Air for

eventual spares use. One airframe, SU-ALL, never left Egypt, being stripped for spares where it stood.

The second major order from the Middle East came from the Lebanon-based Middle East Airlines which contracted for four aircraft in 1959. MEA received its first aircraft

SU-ALL is taxiing out for departure and this nice clear shot reveals the plethora of wing-mounted vents, intakes, and exhausts needed for the protection of the Comet's systems. (Ray Deacon)

5X-AAO is a Comet 4 of EAA. The oval windows fitted to the type from the Comet 2 onward are clearly seen here. (C P Russell Smith Collection)

28 December 1968 were to prove. As part of an operation to curb terrorist activity, the Israeli armed forces inserted a commando team into the airport at Beirut. The resultant operation saw the destruction of three of the Comets plus five other aircraft either owned or leased to MEA.

Fortunately for MEA, Kuwait Airways had just retired its Comet fleet and they were therefore available for immediate lease. These aircraft were flown by MEA until mid-1969 when they were returned to Kuwait, the last to arrive being 9K-ACE in July. This marked the end of Comet operations for MEA which moved on to operate American equipment.

Another Middle East customer was the aforementioned Kuwait Airways which ordered two of the 4C variants in 1962. The first aircraft, 9K-ACE, was delivered in January 1963 although there was a year's gap

in December 1960, the other three followed in the first part of the following year. A fifth airframe built against an MEA option was not taken up due to the airline's financial problems. It was, however, completed and eventually sold to Aerolineas Argentinas. Once the new airliner was established, the airline opened routes from Lebanon that touched Europe, the Middle East, and the Indian subcontinent.

They were a very unfortunate organisation as events on the night of

Seen from a three-quarter front-on angle this Comet 4, 9K-ACI, of Kuwait Airways displays the slight outward and downward angles built into the aircraft's intakes. (C P Russell Smith Collection)

Being towed toward the departure stand is Comet 4C ST-AAX of Sudan Airways. As the Comet was devoid of an APU, battery power was used to display brake system pressures. (C P Russell Smith Collection)

between deliveries. A third airframe, a Comet 4, was added in December 1966 when an ex-BOAC aircraft, G-APDN, was purchased. In common with other Middle East operators, Kuwait Airways soon opened up routes to other Arab States, Europe, and the Indian subcontinent.

The type's sojourn in Kuwait was short in nature as they were all retired from use in 1968 and replaced by the Boeing 707. They were leased for a short time by MEA until sold to Dan Air for further use.

The final airline order of any consequence came from Sudan Airways, which picked up the options on the two lapsed Mexicana aircraft. These were delivered in November and December 1962. Operationally both aircraft were concentrated on the routes into Europe plus more local flights in the Middle East. Although the Sudan was in a perilous financial state the Comets remained active on international flights until the last one was flown out of Heathrow on 11 November 1972. A short period of regional fly-

ing followed before both aircraft were sold to Dan Air.

The final aircraft from the Comet 4C build were both singletons. One was an airframe sold to East African Airways which was delivered on 10 April 1962 as VP-KRL. After nine years of service it was purchased by Dan Air for spares recovery.

The final single airframe was that ordered by the Saudi Royal Flight. Registered SA-R-7 it was delivered on 15 June 1962. Its career with the flight was short-lived as it was lost in a crash over the Italian Alps on 20 March 1963.

Of all the operators who flew the Comet, that of Dan Air has become the most synonymous.

This Chester-built aircraft of EAA is at Heathrow undergoing maintenance as the litter of replenishment trolleys and other equipment demonstrates. (C P Russell Smith Collection)

This Comet 4C, OD-ADR, was delivered to MEA. It was later destroyed in December 1968 when Israeli forces attacked Beirut Airport. (BAE Systems)

Established in 1953 as an offshoot of Davies and Newman with a Douglas DC-3 as its first aircraft, the airline eventually grew to a reasonable size so that by the mid-1960s Airspeed Ambassadors, Bristol Freighters, and more DC-3s were sporting the company's titles.

Dan Air's involvement with the Comet was the result of the burgeoning IT markets in which the company had a healthy stake. The primary problems facing the airline at this point in its history were that of range and speed in its piston-powered fleet. The answer was to switch to jet propulsion.

The first buys were a pair of

In order that aircraft such as the Comet could clear the main door beams of some facilities, the aircraft could be tilted back as shown to drop the fin height. (BAE Systems)

retired BOAC aircraft which were officially purchased in October 1966. The actual transfer had taken place some months earlier to allow the engineering staff at Lasham to convert them to a high-density layout. This internal rearrangement allowed a total of 106 passengers. The first official flight by a Dan Air aircraft, the first of 49 separate airframes, was undertaken in mid-November.

Although the winter period was relatively slow, a total contrast to today's scenario, both Comets, G-APDK and "DO," were to be utilised to the full during the 1967 summer season. Such was the success of these first aircraft that plans were quickly drawn up to purchase two more aircraft, G-APDJ and "DN," plus a flight simulator from the same source.

Although the IT and charter markets are notable for their volatility, on occasion the Comets already in service proved to be great assets to the airline and its operations. It therefore spent the next few years buying surplus Comets at a steady rate from other operators upgrading their fleets. In order to cope with the holiday traffic, Dan Air and the tour operators flew from airports all over the UK. Thus aircraft bearing the Dan Air titling could be seen arriving and departing from Gatwick, Manchester, Birmingham, Newcastle, Teeside, and Luton. At the other end of the route the destinations could include many of the Spanish resorts plus airfields in Greece.

Having bought up the fleets of MSA and EAA the airline turned its attention to Aerolineas Argentinas to further increase its Comet fleet. These were quickly followed by airframes from Kuwait and further examples from EAA. All were flown to Lasham either for upgrading or for reduction to spares. A similar fate also befell those aircraft that had

Undergoing essential engine maintenance with its doors lowered is this Comet 4, 9V-BAS, of MSA. (C P Russell Smith Collection)

started Dan Air in the jet charter field. From 1971 to late 1973 the ex-BOAC machines were withdrawn on a one-for-one basis for spares recovery and eventual scrapping.

Further airframes in Comet 4B form were the next variant in the sights of Dan Air. During 1972-73, the company successfully purchased the retired fleets of BEA, Air Tours, and Channel Airways. Eventually 15 aircraft of this marque passed through the engineering base at Lasham; two were spares recovered, the rest were thrown into the fray to cope with the ever-expanding holiday flight market.

This sort of intensive flying has marked effects on an already high time airframe. Thus by 1975 the airline was already retiring the Comet 4Bs due to high hours and fatigue index consumption. The final in-service flight by one of these veterans was undertaken on 23 October 1975 when G-APYD completed its sched-

Steps away, chocks away, and power cover closed, the crew chief prepares to disconnect as OD-ADS, a Comet 4C of MEA, prepares to depart. Of note is the long aerial wire stretching from the fin to the mid fuselage. (C P Russell Smith Collection)

The first replacements for the retired 4B fleet were the five RAF machines, all of the 4C variant, once the pride of the 216th Squadron. With low airframe hours and fatigue index consumption they were a complete bargain at £120,000 each. Further airframes were also purchased from Sudan Airways and Egyptair although the latter were purchased for spares. One of the Comets was in fact stripped of anything usable at Cairo as it was deemed unfit to fly.

With its flaps drooped, possibly due to dispersion of hydraulic pressure, retired N888WA, had once flown in Mexicana colours. (Jennifer M Gradidge Collection)

uled Gatwick-Crete-Gatwick run. A week later this last operational member of the marque made its final flight to the Science Museum base at Wroughton. After final shutdown it was calculated that the aircraft had completed 32,738 flying hours coupled to which were 18,586 landings. One other Comet 4B survived with Dan Air at Gatwick although this was a working airframe being used for ground handling training.

Once at Lasham, the Dan Air engineering base, the aircraft were prepared for service. The ex-RAF Comets, however, required extra work to change them from their military configuration to a civilian one. Also a requirement to modify or frequently inspect an area of the front spar had become necessary thus slowing their entry into service.

One of the most prestigious orders received by DH was from the Saudi Royal Flight. Registered as SA-R-7, this Comet was to be lost in a crash over the Alps. As this photo shows from its higher viewpoint, the wing root dinghies were located under the light-coloured panels, which had a reputation of being difficult to fit. (BAE Systems)

The last group of passengers are about to board Comet 4, 9V-BAU, of Malaysian Airways. Once all are onboard much of the surrounding ground equipment will be removed. (Jennifer M Gradidge Collection)

This final batch of Comets began to trickle into usage from 1975 and was to provide sterling service to the airline for the next five years. However, the writing was on the wall for the venerable Comet as Dan Air was purchasing examples of the Boeing 727 with a forecast that the 737, and later the Airbus, would eventually appear under Dan Air titles. This upgrading of the Dan Air operational fleet foresaw the last four Comets retiring in 1980. To confirm this fact an enthusiast's special was flown on 9 November to close out the type's illustrious career.

That final flight by G-BDIW was destined to be the last commercial Comet flight in the world although examples would carry on operating in military marks for a few years longer. Of the five machines extant at the end of Comet operations, one went to BAE at Bitteswell for Nimrod development work, one was to be scrapped, whilst the other three were preserved.

The merger of Malaysian Airways and Singapore Airline resulted in the creation of MSA. This is 9M-AOD, belonging to the new organisation. (Jennifer M Gradidge Collection)

Seen not long after leaving MSA service is Comet 4, G-APDM, parked at Lasham awaiting conversion to the configuration required by Dan Air. (C P Russell Smith Collection)

Comet 4C, G-AYVS, was originally delivered to Kuwait Airways. When acquired by Dan Air it was painted in the company's first colour scheme which included highlighting the overwing escape points. (C P Russell Smith Collection)

On the stand at Gatwick is Comet 4, G-APDJ, being prepared for flight. The cabin crew is already boarding as one of the ground handlers begins the removal of the number 2 ECU intake blank. (C P Russell Smith Collection)

IN GLORIOUS COLOUR

Civil airliners have become very much the artists' canvas since air travel became established after the last global conflict. However not for De Havilland and the other early Comet operators the wild excesses of the British Airways ethnic tail art nor the wild colourful meanderings of a Braniff, this was the austerity period and the finishes reflected their times.

Those early airliners were therefor austere in their colour schemes with a basic white cabin set over a polished airframe which sufficed for most, with cheat lines and fins reflecting house colours. Thus, BOAC used regal blue offset by a speedbird motif high upon the fin. The French carriers opted for a similar scheme although all this came to naught once the problems that were to afflict the early aircraft came to light.

It took the Comet to reach version four before airline colours appeared once more. First again came BOAC, though it was joined in the UK by BEA which applied red and black in various parts to the wings and fin. A spread of smaller airlines also flew the Comet from the shores of Britain although none would become as famous as the last Comet operator, Dan Air whose fleet sported various plays upon the company house colours of red and white.

Overseas customers for the aircraft played their part in the evolution of the Comet as a canvas. Gone from the repertoire of the airlines outside Europe were the cold blues of more temperate climes. Their Comets were of a far more colourful nature with yellows and greens predominating all, offset by black highlights and shading. Although the Comet no longer graces the skies of the world, some of these finishes can still be seen upon those preserved airframes that are still with us.

On the other hand the Comets of the military were austere to the point of anonymity. White and light grey were their colours, and in the case of the 'radio calibration' aircraft this was a form of reverse camouflage. In the days of the Nimrod, the final evolution of the Comet, the situation became even more drab with the white giving way to a hemp colour. Although in recent years, brightly coloured fins and other special marks have been allowed. Only the test and evaluation organisations have brought splashes of colour to the other Comets in military marks. Bright red fins and other marking have coloured these airframes out of the ordinary and this sight may be repeated in the UK at least when the last Comet to fly, *Canopus*, hopefully returns to flying status in 2001.

Comet 4, LV-PLM, of Aerolineas Argentinas passes by the camera aircraft on a pre-delivery sortie. Of note is the highly polished finish of the unpainted portions of the aircraft. (BAE Systems)

Sudan Airways Comet 4C, ST-AAW, was originally laid down for a Mexicana order. Due to financial difficulties this airline failed to exercise its option, thus the aircraft was sold to Sudan. It eventually finished its long career as a spares source for the Dan Air fleet. (BAE Systems)

This particular Comet is the second airframe to have been allocated to BOAC as G-APDJ. The first was diverted by agreement to Aerolineas Argentinas. (Huw Bowen Collection)

From the outset the DH Ghost engine was viewed as an interim powerplant which would be replaced by the Avon once sufficient numbers became available. (Marc Schaeffer)

Registered as 9K-ACA by Kuwait Airways in December 1962, this particular Comet spent time with MEA after its aircraft were destroyed by Israeli forces. In common with many similar aircraft it ended its days with Dan Air. (Mel James)

In its day the cockpit of the Comet was considered quite modern, although comparison with that of the Nimrod will reveal that some significant changes have taken place. (Marc Schaeffer)

SU-AMV was a Comet 4C registered to United Arab Airlines. Upon dissolution of this organisation it became Egyptair property before final disposal to Dan Air. (Huw Bowen Collection)

Now wearing BEA Airtours' livery for the tourist market, Comet 4B G-ARGM had originally been part of the fleet list for the parent company BEA. (Huw Bowen Collection)

Originally ordered for BOAC as G-AMXJ, this Comet 2 later became a C2, XK697, with the 216 Sqdn RAF with whom it was named Cygnus. (Mel James)

The first Comet 4 for BOAC, G-APDA, is seen here flying over southern England not long after departing London's Heathrow airport. Clearly visible in this view is the subtle smooth blending of the aircraft's shape, a feature of all marques of Comet. (BAE Systems)

Once registered as G-APDI of BOAC this Comet 4 later became HC-ALT of Aerovias Ecuatorianas. (Huw Bowen Collection)

DH Comet 1 G-ALYX, of BOAC, first flew on 18 September 1951. After the type's C of A was withdrawn the aircraft was stored until sold to the MoS. It ended its days as a structural test specimen at RAE Farnborough. (Capt. Peter Duffey via Chris Duffey)

Wearing the final scheme sported by the aircraft of Dan Air is Comet 4C ,G-AYVG which is preparing to depart Gatwick. (Mel James Collection)

This smart looking Comet is 5H-AAF of East African Airways preparing to depart from London Heathrow for the Journey home. (Jennifer M Gradidge Collection)

Middle East Airways Comet 4C sports a red cheat line and trimmings to contrast against the otherwise bland silver and white scheme. On the fin the aircraft sports the stylised Cedar Tree of the Lebanon. (Jennifer M Gradidge Collection)

In front of an appreciative audience the last flying Comet 4 XS235 Canopus of the A&AEE flies by with everything out and down. After retirement the aircraft was flown to Bruntingthorpe although plans are afoot to transfer the aircraft to Lasham for a return to flying status. (BBA Collection)

Complete with Nimrod AEW3 aerodynamic test radome and an extended Nimrod fin assembly Comet 4 (mod) XW626 is towed to its parking slot. (Mel James)

The Nimrod AEW3 was an attempt to create an airborne early warning aircraft using some spare Nimrod anti submarine aircraft. From the outset the experiment failed as it proved impossible to fit all the required equipment and cooling systems into such a small airframe; plus a full fuel load placed excessive strain on the undercarriage units. Eventually all 11 aircraft ended up stored at RAF Abingdon to await disposal. (BBA Collection)

In its earliest guise the Nimrod MR.1 was painted in a light grey scheme with white uppersurfaces and lacked all the improvements and refinements associated with the MR.2 upgrade. (BBA Collection)

Pictured side by side are the Comet 4 XS235 Canopus and a standard Nimrod MR.2. The obvious family resemblance shows quite clearly. (BBA Collection)

Just prior to the Falklands war in 1982 the RAF began to paint the Nimrod fleet in a new paint scheme which consisted of Hemp uppersurfaces over light grey undersurfaces. (BBA Collection)

COMETS FOR 5 THE MILITARY

It appears to be almost incumbent today that the nation producing a new transport would be the first to ensure that its armed forces were equipped with it. However, in the case of the DH Comet this was not to be the case.

The first military order for the Comet in the shape of the 1A version came from the Royal Canadian Air Force which had formulated a requirement for two aircraft for high-speed transit and VIP use. Serialled 5301 and 5302 the order was placed with De Havilland in 1952. The first of the pair made its maiden flight on 21 February 1953 being followed by the second on 25 March. Delivery to Canada was effected on 18 March and 13 April respectively.

Operated by No. 412 Sqdn RCAF, the two airliners were both affected by the disasters that struck the early Comets. In light of this they were extensively structurally modified during 1957 to emerge as Comet 1XBs in September after an extended period in storage. Their duties caused them to range all over Canada and North America and occasionally beyond from their base at Uplands, Ontario. Both remained in frontline service until withdrawn on 3 October 1964. During their years of service they had amassed over 11,000 hours flying time covering over 4 million route miles.

The Royal Air Force finally joined the jet transport age when the major portion of the Comet 2 production run was acquired for service. In use the Comets were employed in two completely contrasting roles. One covered basic transport needs whilst the other was engaged in far more clandestine activities.

As previously mentioned the first build Comet 2s had already been completed in 1953. Assigned civil registrations on behalf of BOAC they had already completed their flight testing when the order was cancelled. After a period in storage at Hatfield the first aircraft for the RAF, once G-AMXB, was assigned to No. 216 Sqdn in 1956 as a Comet T.2 for aircrew conversion training. Its period as a trainer was short-lived as it was quickly assigned to the RAF Handling Squadron for the compilation of the type's Pilot's Notes and other data.

A month later, in August, the Comet had returned to the operational strength of 216 Sqdn. Its period of usage, still as a conversion trainer, was also short-lived as the aircraft was to be returned to De Havilland for conversion to full C2 status. Part

Wearing the titles of RCAF Air Transport Command is this Comet 1A serialled 5301. Of note is the open DV window at the captain's position. (Jennifer M Gradidge Collection)

A unique formation photograph of a pair of Comet C2s and a Comet C4 all of No. 216 Sqdn RAF, probably marking the retirement of the former. This view allows a good comparison between the short fuselage of the earlier aircraft and the final build of the Comet. (Jennifer M Gradidge Collection)

of this entailed the refitting of the cabin to carry 48 passengers in rear-ward facing seats and the installation of military compatible avionics.

The first operational Comet C.Mk.2 to be delivered to No. 216 Sqdn was the second of the order,

XK670, which arrived at Lyneham on 7 June 1956. The full fleet of 10 was to be delivered over the following 12 months. The last airframe to be delivered was XK716 which arrived on 7 May 1957 and was the first complete airframe to be rolled

out of the new De Havilland plant at Chester. As the fleet strength built up, the air and ground crews of the squadron settled into the task of learning their new mounts' requirements. Such was their success that the first Transport Command operational sortie, to Moscow, was undertaken on 23 June 1956 which conveyed a party of government officials for trade talks.

From that point the aircraft were increasingly used to convey VIPs across the world, but also found increasing usage as troop and family transport for troops departing overseas. Destinations touched by the squadron's aircraft included the bases in Cyprus, Malta, and other points throughout the Middle and Far East. Europe and 2TAF in West Germany also saw regular Comet flights as did the United States which was visited regularly on a scheduled run, a practise that continues today with the squadron's

This later shot of 5301 shows it to have been reworked to Comet 1XB standard, the most obvious change being the type of cabin window fitted. (C P Russell Smith Collection)

current equipment — the Lockheed Tristar. The farthest regular scheduled point reached by the Comets was Adelaide, which routed via El Adam, Singapore, and Darwin amongst other places. The purpose of these visits was to transfer personnel and their equipment to the nuclear testing facility at Woomera.

As well as the regular flights, the Comets of the 216 Sqdn also found themselves engaged in operations in support of the Suez crisis and its aftermath. When British forces withdrew from the Suez Canal Zone they pulled back to Cyprus from whence they were flown home, although the load was reduced to 44 passengers – only due to the extra equipment carried by each man.

Unlike other airliner users, the Royal Air Force has always insisted that its transports could carry a reasonable cargo load. That of the Comet was set at 11,200 lbs., most of which was stored in the forward cabin area. As the original floor of the aircraft was not stressed to take such a load, a modification programme to enhance the structure

Surrounded by ground crew this Comet C4 is being prepared for engine ground runs. After retirement by the RAF, this aircraft became part of the Dan Air fleet. (C P Russell Smith Collection)

was applied to eight of the airframes.

As De Havilland had extended the range and size of the aircraft to produce the Comet 4 series, the MoS contracted the company to provide six airframes to 4C standard. Five of these aircraft were to be added to the fleet strength of the 216 Sqdn whilst the sixth was to find employment with A&AEE.

The first Comet 4C for the RAF was the Chester-built XR395, which undertook its maiden flight on 15 November 1961. Deliveries of the aircraft, by now designated the Comet C.Mk.4, began to the 216th Squadron at Lyneham on 15 February 1962 when XR397 was taken on charge. XR397 was the first aircraft retained for use as a conversion trainer with the RAF Handling Squadron for the compilation of the

Complete with various lumps, bumps, and the necessary aerials is this Comet C2(R), XK655. Originally ordered as a Comet 2 for BOAC it was later converted for use by No. 192 Sqdn, later to become No. 51 Sqdn. (Jennifer M Gradidge Collection)

This Comet C2(R) shows another variation of the blisters and aerials fitted to these machines. Unlike their passenger-carrying siblings of No. 216 Sqdn these aircraft flew unpressurised. (C P Russell Smith Collection)

Pilot's Notes and other paperwork.

From that point deliveries continued at a steady rate, each aircraft arriving at approximately four-month intervals. In common with the earlier C2 the new aircraft also featured rearward facing passenger seats for 94 persons plus military specified avionics. Once fully integrated into the squadron's structure, the new Comets took over many of the long-haul routes previously assigned to the earlier aircraft. They in turn began operating on the more short-haul flights to destinations in Germany and the Middle East.

The longer range Comet C.4s were tasked to cover the flights to the United States and to the Far East, Hong Kong having been added to the schedule of flights. Royal duties were also another area in which the squadron excelled as the aircraft retained a special royal cabin fit which could be installed in any of the squadron's new aircraft. Away from the glamour of the royal life the aircraft were also employed on trooping flights for which purpose 86 fully loaded personnel could be accommodated.

Together the two breeds of Comet remained operational until 1967 when the C2s were withdrawn, the final service flight being undertaken by XK698 on 1 April. After withdrawal, the aircraft first found use as instructional airframes before being dispersed to other locations.

The remaining five Comets of 216 Sqdn were left to carry the burden alone until the Vickers VC-10 entered service with the 10th Squadron in July 1966. The De Havilland product, however, retained its

XK695 was allocated to No. 51 Sqdn for what the Defence White Paper called "radio and radar calibration trials." (C P Russell Smith Collection)

schedules as its range was slightly longer than that of the newer Vickers product.

Governments are always keen to make irrational defence cuts in times of peace. One victim of such pruning was 216 Sqdn and its Comets. In 1975 plans were announced in the defence white paper to reduce significantly the size of Support Command, the organisation that had replaced the earlier Transport Command. This decision flew in the face of the Command's planners who had ascertained that the Comet's life in the RAF would continue until at least 1980 due in part to the average monthly flying time for each airframe being no more than 300 hours

per month. This meant that the squadron undertook its final VIP flight in April 1975 with regular services stopping soon after.

Upon withdrawal the aircraft were flown to Leconfield for the removal of military-sourced items before being offered for resale. Dan Air was to be the purchaser of these aircraft which had an excellent working life left; as they had only flown an average of 11,500 hours, deemed as only 40 percent of total time available. One airframe did eventually return to quasi-military use, this being G-BDIU which had once been XR396. Purchased by BAe after withdrawal by Dan Air the aircraft was transferred to HSA

Bitteswell where it was used in the Nimrod development programme.

The other Royal Air Force operator of the Comet was No. 192 Sqdn, later to evolve into 51 Sqdn. This unit's role in life had been identified as "radio and radar calibration" and the first postwar equipment had been specially modified Boeing Washington bombers, better known as the B-29 Superfortress. The need to enter the jet age in the ELINT field had been identified as necessary by 1955. Thus on 23 February, the MoS had been approached to provide one Comet 2 minus engines which would have a minimum fatigue life of 2,000 hours. To enable quick introduction into service it

Seen from underneath is this Comet C2 that was assigned to 216 Sqdn for use in a transport role. On the early build aircraft the pitot heads were carried out on the wingtip whilst on the later models they had been moved to the forward fuselage. (C P Russell Smith Collection)

Before the RAF would accept the Comet 2 the aircraft had to undergo rigorous testing to obviate the chance of any failure in the fuselage structure. (C P Russell Smith Collection)

The unpainted skin of this Comet C2 reveals the layout of the fuselage structure clearly. (C P Russell Smith Collection)

When the Comets entered RAF service they were designated T2s. After conversion they were redesignated C2s. The two most obvious changes were the installation of rearward facing seats and military standard avionics. (Ray Deacon)

was agreed that the RAF would accept the aircraft in original BOAC condition and modify as required to suit the new role.

The first airframe, formerly G-AMXE, first flew on 18 July. It was powered by GFE powerplants, these being the uprated RR Avon 504s rated at 7,330 lbs.st. Other equipment fitted included Marconi AB107B/114 HF radio, Marconi 7092B ADF, STR14B/15B ILS, Murphy Mk6 200m/c DME, Ultra UA17 intercom, Sperry ZL1 zero-reader, a periscope sextant, escape equipment, and smoke masks. As the fuselage was built to the original specification and still retained square windows, the cabin pressurisation system was removed.

The second and third aircraft were contracted soon after this and emerged from Marshalls of Cambridge as XK655 and XK659 in April and August 1957 respectively to join XK663, the original aircraft. Upon entry into service the three aircraft

Comet 1A XM823 had once been operated by Air France as F-BGNZ. When returned to DH it was reworked to 1XB standard and used for trials purposes. (Capt. Peter Duffey via Chris Duffey)

were designated C.Mk2(RC). Changes to the flight deck were minimal, only GFE being fitted to change the layout slightly.

For RAF purposes a flight crew of four was carried as standard; comprising of two pilots, a navigator, and a flight engineer. It was in the main cabin, however, that the

greatest changes had taken place. Gone were the seats of the standard passenger fit; in their place stood racks of black boxes dedicated to the ELINT role. To nurse these new occupants, a dedicated team was deployed consisting of eight operatives, later increased to 10, and two supervisors.

Awaiting its next crew is Comet T2, XK697. This designation was applied to the aircraft when they were first supplied as they were still in basic civilian configuration. (C P Russell Smith Collection)

Seen at a later date, Comet 2E XN453 is festooned with blisters and aerials for its trials roles. (Ray Deacon)

Entry into service began when XK663 was declared ready for collection on 17 April 1957. Two days later it was ferried to Watton for final fitting before assuming operations with the 192 Sqdn. The second airframe, XK659, came on line at Watton in March 1958, being closely followed by XK655. Within months No. 192 Sqdn had been renumbered as 51 Sqdn.

Although much of 51 Sqdn's work is still shrouded in secrecy, it is reported that the squadron's aircraft were seen quite regularly in Norway, Cyprus, and Kenya.

A change to the squadron's strength occurred in 1959 when another aircraft was required to replace XK663 which had been destroyed in a hangar fire on 3 June. Such was the urgency for replacement that XK695, a fully modified Comet C2 of 216 Sqdn, was with-

Wearing the title of RAF Transport Command this 216 Sqdn Comet C2 is parked and awaiting its next sortie. (C P Russell Smith Collection)

Once registered as G-AMXD for BOAC this airframe was later modified to Comet 2E standard after which it was turned over to the MoS for trials work. (Capt. Peter Duffey via Chris Duffey)

Except for the reversal of the seating and the installation of military avionics there was little difference between the Comet 4C and C4. (C P Russell Smith Collection)

The arrival of the Comet 4C to 216 Sqdn enabled the RAF to move more people farther and faster. (Jennifer M Gradidge Collection)

drawn from Transport Command operations and ferried to Marshalls of Cambridge for full conversion.

Withdrawals of the "special" Comets began in 1974 when the two original survivors were no longer on the active flying inventory. The replacements for the Comets were three reworked Nimrods, which joined the 51st Squadron during the period 1974–75.

This, however, was not the end of the Comet in military marks as A&AEE and the RAE found the aircraft suited their needs admirably as a transport and testbed. The first Comets in military marks were two of the Air France Mk.1 examples, F-BGNY and "NZ." These became XM829 and "823" respectively. The former was employed for Decca Doppler trials amongst other trials whilst the latter was used on behalf of the research organisations by HS

Dynamics, once DH Props, for unspecified trials work.

A pair of Comet 2 aircraft also wore military serials. Designated as Comet 2Es these were the former G-AMXD and "XK" which appeared as XN453 and XV144 respectively. Both were extensively used in the field of avionics development. In the case of XN453, its first task was the testing of long-range radio systems whilst the other Comet 2E was

The deployment of this Comet C2's flaps highlights the location of the fuel dump pipes on the surface's trailing edge. Connection from the wing to the moving portion was by reinforced flexible hose. XK715 remained in RAF service until 1966. (C P Russell Smith Collection)

Not often seen on the Comet is the tail support rod that screws into the tail bumper. This particular aircraft is being used for instructional duties at RAF Halton and needs additional support as students walk through the parked aircraft. (Jennifer M Gradidge Collection)

The Comets in RAF service required long-range UHF communications, which was catered for by the long aerial wire stretching from the fuselage to the top of the fin. (C P Russell Smith Collection)

Sitting on the hot concrete pan at Sharjah it is surprising that there are no cabin conditioning blowers blasting cool air into the cabin. The only GSE item plugged in is the power supply set. (C P Russell Smith Collection)

Cleaning up after takeoff this shot of XM823 shows the "D" doors cycling through after the main gears have retracted. (C P Russell Smith Collection)

extensively engaged in Smith's Autopilot trials from 1966 onward.

The most unique aircraft in the lineup was the sole Comet 3, which had acted as the development vehicle for the Comet 4 series. For this purpose it was registered G-ANLO. After completing its civil develop-ment trials the aircraft was purchased in 1961 for use in blind landing experiments for which purpose it was designated XP915. Operated by the BLEU at RAE Bedford the aircraft was later employed on runway braking tests. This involved high-speed taxi runs down the runway to test the effectiveness of various retardants in an effort to develop a method of stopping an aircraft with braking and/or undercarriage problems. From the brake trials, XP915 was transferred to BAE Woodford in 1978 for Nimrod AEW3 development work.

Except for a coat of paint there was very little difference between the civilian and military Comets. This is the reason why Dan Air was keen to buy the RAF machines when they were retired. Compared to a civilian counterpart, the RAF fleet had flown very low hours in its military career. (C P Russell Smith Collection)

Escorted by two Lightning F3s of No. 56 Sqdn this Comet C4, XR396, is inbound to Akrotiri, Cyprus. (John Nickolls)

As expected, the biggest group of Comets in use as testbeds came from the Comet 4 series, a total of five being employed on such duties. Three of the airframes had already flown quite extensively for BOAC before purchase by the MoS. The aircraft had been G-APDF, "DS," and "DP" before re-designation as XV814, XW626, and XX944. Of the three XX944 was only in use for a short time for unspecified duties before returning to the civil market with Dan Air.

Comet 4 XV814 remained in active use for many years after joining RAE. Its final series of trials before withdrawal in 1992 covered Nimrod development trials for which

purpose it sported a Nimrod fin, rudder, and fintip ESM pod. The other Comet 4, XW626, had undergone handling trials with the A&AEE before passing to BAE Woodford for conversion into the Nimrod AEW3 aerodynamic prototype. The major alteration to the airframe was the fitment of an enormous proboscis designed to contain the nose scanner for this abortive project. Flight trials were completed by August 1981 after which the airframe was stored at Bedford before being scrapped.

Two other Comets of the 4C variety were also engaged on Nimrod trials. These were the partially completed airframes of the final civil Comet production that had been

placed in storage when no customers were forthcoming. Emerging in 1967 the first of these, XV147, became the avionics development vehicle for the MR1 and 2 versions of the anti-submarine patrol aircraft. As full type performance was not required, XV147 was powered by Avon engines which it retained right up until withdrawal in August 1981.

The other airframe took longer to emerge as it was intended as a full-flight test vehicle for which purpose RR Spey engines, destined for the production Nimrod, were fitted. This entailed some reconstruction of the engine bay area to accommodate the bigger powerplant, thus it was not until May 1967 that XV148 first flew. In addition to its duties as an aerodynamic testbed the aircraft was also used for weapons development and deployment before final withdrawal in the 1980s.

The final Comet in this survey is XS235 which had been purchased as the sixth aircraft in the Comet 4C buy. The other five served with 216 Sqdn whilst XS235 began active service with A&AEE in December 1963. Named *Canopus*, the aircraft was first flown to Boscombe Down where extensive racking for avionics equipment was installed. Intended as a development testbed for radio, radar, and navigation systems the aircraft also featured an extensive selection of camera windows in the belly for use in the development of reconnaissance cameras.

First experiments concerning *Canopus* involved Decca Doppler navigation equipment for which purpose a large fairing was installed under the forward fuselage. The accuracy of this system enabled the aircraft to undertake a record-breaking series of flights in 1968. Integrated with the Doppler radar were a pair of INS platforms, which successfully guided the aircraft on a round-the-world east-about flight during July and August. A further flight was undertaken in May 1969 although this time the route was west about. Having proved the validity of the INS as an accurate navigation unit, the big test came in September when the Comet flew over the Magnetic North Pole to see the effects that transpired. Although compasses go totally haywire when over this source the INS platforms restrained themselves to a gentle twitching. Further flight trials at the end of the year during "Exercise Canopus" saw Loran "C" and Omega navigation aids fitted. This series of flights finally proved the worth of a fully integrated navigation system capable of taking its cues from both internal and external sources.

As XS235 was dedicated purely to avionics work it comes as no surprise to find that it was extensively involved in the systems development for the Nimrod MR1 and 2 during the 1980s. At the close of the decade, *Canopus* was fitted with the GPS Navstar system to take part in the international test programme. During this period the aircraft visited Thule, Greenland, from where it regularly flew over the North Pole.

XS235 was to finally retire on 14 March 1997, after its final service flight, as it became scheduled for a major servicing. Given the age of the aircraft and paucity of spares it was decided by the MOD that retirement was a better option. Originally the aircraft was placed in the MOD auction catalogue scheduled for May. Pressure was exerted on MOD from

Comet 4 (mod) XV814 was the penultimate flying member of the class. Once G-APDF of BOAC, some of the modifications carried out by the RAE are clearly visible. (Jennifer M Gradidge Collection)

Seen directly from underneath, this shot of Canopus *reveals the fully extended flap area.* (BBA Collection)

many quarters that indicated that preservation was the preferred end for this, the last of the Comets.

Initially Hatfield was suggested as the aircraft's final resting place although this was soon discounted when it was revealed that the airfield was to be disposed of and the runway was covered in speed bumps to stop illegal car racing. The aircraft's final resting place was chosen as Bruntingthorpe in the care of British Aviation Heritage. XS235 made its, and the Comet's, final flight in October, thus bringing an end to a turbulent era.

Possibly the most celebrated Comet is the XS235 Canopus *seen here with everything out and down for landing.* (BBA Collection)

After the failure of the Comet 1 in service, the follow-on order for the Comet 2 for BOAC was cancelled. The greater majority of the redundant airframes were reworked and passed onto 216 Sqdn for transport duties. Of the remainder some were fitted with specialist ELINT systems whilst others joined the various test fleets. (C P Russell Smith Collection)

This side-on view of a Comet C2 of 216 Sqdn reveals a feature much copied in current airliner development, the steeply contoured nose which not only reduces airframe drag, but makes rain dispersal more efficient. (C P Russell Smith Collection)

This picture shows XM829, once of the A&AEE, sitting on the firepan at Stanstead Airport. The removal of the tailplanes has revealed the mounting points and the location for the tailplane de-icing duct. (C P Russell Smith Collection)

AIRLINER**TECH**
SERIES

On a departure flyby XP915 reveals the nose probe more clearly in this view. (Jennifer M Gradidge Collection)

Parked at Farnborough is Comet 3 XP915. Of note are the modifications to this airframe. The first is the extended nose probe blended into the forward fuselage whilst the second is purely cosmetic consisting of photographic target marks on the cabin roof. (Ray Deacon)

Parked at Lyneham is this Comet C2, XK670, of No. 216 Sqdn. The prominent wing fences on the early marque Comets were required to straighten the airflow over the ailerons. (C P Russell Smith Collection)

XK699 Sagittarius was a Comet C2 allocated to 216 Sqdn. When the series 2 Comets were planned, their fuselage featured improved structural strength and the replacement of the early square windows with oval ones. (Ray Deacon)

XK716 is pictured in earlier days at Lyneham on the strength of 216 Sqdn. Under the nose is a set of oxygen bottles that have been used to replenish the crew's emergency supply. (C P Russell Smith Collection)

THE ULTIMATE COMET

NIMROD AND THE DEVELOPMENT AIRCRAFT

The requirement for the Nimrod came about due to the need of the RAF to replace its original anti-submarine and patrol aircraft, the Avro Shackleton. Developed from the wartime Lancaster, the Shackleton, although reliable, was slow and was not capable of further development.

The answer put forward by Hawker Siddeley Aviation was a development of the Comet airliner. It was seen as a more viable alternative to an aircraft such as the Lockheed P-3 Orion, which lacked the speed for short-range dash missions.

Planning for the new aircraft began in 1966 and resulted in a contract being awarded for two development prototypes that were to be based upon the last two uncompleted Comet 4 airframes.

Designated XV147 and XV148, the two aircraft flew in 1967. The first airframe was powered by the original RR Avon turbojets but was aerodynamically correct otherwise. Major structural changes included the double bubble fuselage, the lower portion of which contained the weapons bay, and a shortened nose leg complete with modified gear doors. The rear fuselage also came in for some attention as it gained a new fin complete with ESM pod. The final change to the rear fuselage was the addition of a MAD boom. As this entailed an increase in overall all up weight, the main gear units and supporting structure were strengthened to cope.

Dimensionally the Nimrod is similar to the preceding Comet. The wingspan was set at 114 ft. 10 in. with a fuselage length set at 126 ft. 9 in. for the MR versions. The production aircraft are fitted with RR Spey 250 RB168-20 turbofans rated at 12,160 lbs.st. each. Basic maximum all up weight is set at 177,500 lbs. with an overload capability of 192,000 lbs. Maximum speed is 575 mph (500 kts) with cruising speed set at 490 mph (425 kts), although on long patrols the outboard engines are shut down.

When needed, the idling powerplants can be restarted to allow for short-term dash speeds. Range without in-flight refueling is set between 5,180 and 5,755 miles giving an endurance of some 12 hours. One of the useful extras built into the Nimrod's starboard wing tank is a one million-candlepower searchlight which has proved useful when the aircraft is scrambled for SAR missions. Under all conditions the Nimrod is crewed by three on the flight deck and 13 system operators in the main cabin.

The second prototype, XV148, was rebuilt to full HS801 standard

Parked side by side are XS235 and a Nimrod MR2. The family resemblance is readily apparent. (BBA Collection)

complete with RR Spey engines that featured thrust reversers on the outboard installations. This aircraft made its maiden flight from Chester on 23 May 1967, the other aircraft, XV147, departed Woodford on 31 July. Once the aerodynamic test flying had been completed, avionics integration testing began. Fortunately many of the systems fitted to the HS801, by now named Nimrod, were developments of the equipment fitted to the Shackleton.

An initial contract for the first production batch of aircraft, totaling 38 in all, was placed even as the prototypes were test flying. Thus on 28 June 1968 XV226 departed Woodford on its maiden flight. Deliveries started from this point, the first recipient being the MOTU later to be renumbered as 236 OCU at St. Maw-gan, which received its first aircraft in October 1969.

Further deliveries were to units that had originally operated the venerable Shackleton, these being No. 120, 201, and 206 Sqdns at Kinloss. Joining the OCU at St. Mawgan was No. 42 Sqdn which received its first Nimrod on 3 April 1971. Overseas No. 203 Sqdn based in Luqa, Malta, began to re-equip with the Nimrod MR1 on 31 July 1971 for Mediterranean patrols.

A further eight aircraft were ordered as attrition spares in January 1972. First flights began in 1974 by which time the need for the aircraft had passed as the RAF had begun to withdraw from Luqa and other bases as part of extensive peacetime defence cuts.

Rationalisation of the UK aircraft industry saw the creation of British Aerospace in 1977. This corporation absorbed both BAC and Hawker Siddeley and thus became the parent organisation for the Nimrod. Hawker Siddeley had already begun the development work on the advanced avionics suite that would feature quite heavily in the MR2 upgrade programme. Test flying began using XV148 on 23 June 1976.

Three Nimrods were also involved with the development work and began test flying in March 1978, May 1978, and March 1979 respectively. The latter aircraft had in fact taken to the air after the first conversion had been test flown in February before delivery to No. 201 Sqdn on 23 August.

A total of 35 airframes eventually underwent conversion to the new

The venerable Shackleton AEW 2 can trace its ancestry back to the Lancaster bomber of World War II vintage. The radome under the nose, which contains the radar scanner, is not much younger as the earliest examples first flew under the Grumman Avenger. (BBA Collection)

This nose-on view of a Nimrod MR2 shows that this final development of the DH106 design retained much of the original. (BBA Collection)

One area that was modified extensively was the rear fuselage and fin. The former gained a MAD sting whilst the other became more angular and finished with an ESM pod. (BBA Collection)

On the point of touchdown this Nimrod MR2 has been fitted with a refuelling probe that was originally required for operations during the Falklands War. To counteract the changes in aerodynamics caused by this installation, an auxiliary keel and tailplane finlets were required. (BBA Collection)

standard, the final aircraft being handed over in 1985. Changes to the aircraft saw the aircraft's weight growing by 6,000 lbs. The only obvious external changes were the blanking off of a cabin window, some new intakes and ducts on the rear fuselage, and the repositioning of some aerials. Internally the changes had resulted in a major upgrade to the aircraft's primary systems. The original build radar, the ASV Mk.21, had been no more than a revamp of the unit originally fitted to the Shackleton. It was replaced by the far more advanced EMI ARI 5980 Searchwater system. Sonobuoy tracking and signal processing now became the responsibility of twin Marconi AQS 901 units.

Further external changes were wrought due to the Falklands War in 1982. In a bid to extend the Nimrod's range, in-flight refueling probes, removed from redundant Vulcans, were plumbed in above the cabin roof. To compensate for the change in longitudinal stability a ventral fin was added as were finlets on the tailplanes.

Further changes were made to the weapons capability when the fitments and control systems for both AIM-9 Sidewinders and Martel missiles were integrated into the aircraft complete with underwing pylons. Further weapons clearances were obtained for the Marconi Stingray torpedo, 1,000-lb. Hunting BL755 cluster bombs, and the AGM-84A Harpoon missiles. The increased capability meant that the Nimrods could endure sorties that lasted up to 19 hours in duration. After hostilities had ceased, most of the modifications were cleared for normal service usage.

Another variant of the Nimrod was also ordered although no great fanfare was made of the contract, as the three aircraft involved were required for ELINT purposes. Destined for use by No. 51 Sqdn they were to replace the unit's earlier Comets. Designated the R Mk.1, the three aircraft entered squadron service without ceremony in 1974. Differences from their ASW brethren were the removal of the MAD sting and its replacement by a short radome, similar installations were placed at the leading edge of the wing tanks.

As the type's role has developed there have been changes to the equipment fitted. Much of this is classified, therefore only external changes such as the deletion of windows to shield new equipment racks and an increasing aerial farm under the fuselage can be noticed. The Falklands War also saw the introduction of in-flight refueling probes plus associated stability devices to one aircraft for South Atlantic duties, although the modifications were later extended to cover the other two. Further upgrades saw the wingtips being modified to carry Loral ARI 18240 ESM pods before the ASW versions were so equipped.

In-service losses to the Nimrod fleet have been minimal with only two of the MR versions being lost. One was due to a multiple bird

This view of a Nimrod MR2 shows the limited ground clearance available when the weapons bay doors are open. (BBA Collection)

The extent of the Nimrod's weapons bay is visible in this photograph. This cannot only house offensive weapons, but has a further use for SAR equipment during rescue operations. (BBA Collection)

strike on takeoff from Kinloss, the other was caused by control problems during an airshow in Canada. Only one Nimrod R.1 has been lost to date, this being an aircraft on a post-major-test flight that was forced by circumstances to ditch in the North Sea. Such was the importance of the R1 that another aircraft, a Nimrod MR2, was slated for conversion to fill the loss.

The Nimrod that replaced the lost R.1 was made available due to the trimming of the front line fleet during another round of defence cuts. A few aircraft have been withdrawn for spares recovery, but 21 are undergoing a complete rebuild to a new standard. Designated the MR4, the aircraft's wings, tail unit, and engines are replaced by new build items whilst the fuselage undergoes rigorous examination and repair. New mission avionics are courtesy of Boeing and replace the original mainly-British suite. After rebuild the revamped aircraft will be returned to service with the Kinloss wing complete with new serial numbers.

The last variant of the Nimrod to be developed was an airborne early warning version. Originally the UK's AEW presence had been carrier based, although this ceased with the withdrawal of the aircraft carrier HMS *Ark Royal*. To provide much

Banking towards the camera this view of a Nimrod MR2 reveals the extensive changes made from the earlier Comet. Not only were major changes made to the wings, but the rework of the fuselage and fin resulted in a virtually brand new aircraft. (BBA Collection)

needed air defence cover, MOD initiated a conversion programme to graft the radar system from withdrawn Fairey Gannets under the noses of recently withdrawn Shackletons. Due to their age these aircraft were not capable of extensive upgrading. Therefore when it became obvious that the aircraft were ageing beyond further recovery, it was decided to utilise 11 Nimrod airframes that had been in storage since the Defence White Paper of 1975 had begun the contraction of the RAF's theatres of responsibility.

Although the creation of the Nimrod AEW3 was due to expediency it was doomed from the outset. Eleven airframes were chosen for conversion, the most obvious

changes being a large radome at each end of the fuselage. Designed to house the system scanners, the bulbous radomes had been test flown on a testbed Comet 4, XW626. The necessary avionics and processing equipment were housed in the fuselage, thus increasing the weight quite drastically.

Throughout the whole programme it was beset with problems. The increase in gross weight meant that strengthening of the wings and undercarriage was required although this too led to further handling difficulties as it was found that the aircraft had great trouble in taxiing when fully loaded. Malfunctions with the system avionics due to excessive overheating resulted in

problems with the processors which in turn caused detection rates to fall.

After vast amounts of money had been expended upon the project resulting in enormous cost overruns, it was decided to stop. The aircraft were stripped to basic standard and in the main flown to Abingdon for storage. From this Oxfordshire location the airframes were dispersed to various locations for training purposes before eventual scrapping. Instead of the abortive Nimrod, the MOD purchased Boeing AWACS.

Although the last mentioned version of the Nimrod was a complete flop, the rebuilt MR4 will keep the last vestiges of the Comet flying well into the new century some 50 years after its birth.

This view of a Nimrod flight deck reveals that little remains from Comet except the control yoke. (BBA Collection)

Parked awaiting its crew this Nimrod MR2 assigned to the Kinloss wing reveals all the major and minor modifications that were required to create this aircraft from the Comet. (BBA Collection)

This close up of a Nimrod rear fuselage shows the finlets needed for longitudinal stability after the probe was installed plus the intake required to cool the onboard ESM. (BBA Collection)

Once the Nimrod R1s were ready for service, the earlier Comet C2(R) fleet was retired. By this time any pretence at "calibration" had been dropped and the ELINT role acknowledged. (BBA Collection)

Seen on an early test flight from RAF Waddington this Nimrod AEW3 reveals the extent that GEC and BAE had gone through to try to squeeze a quart into a pint pot. (Mel James)

Whilst in storage at Abington the defunct AEW fleet was kept in flyable condition until a decision was made regarding its future. (BBA Collection)

*This close up view of the nose of a Nimrod AEW3 reveals the great changes wrought upon the airframe to create this new variant. Close observation of this airframe reveals that component recovery is well underway. The removed items would then be refurbished for use in the MR2 fleet.
(BBA Collection)*

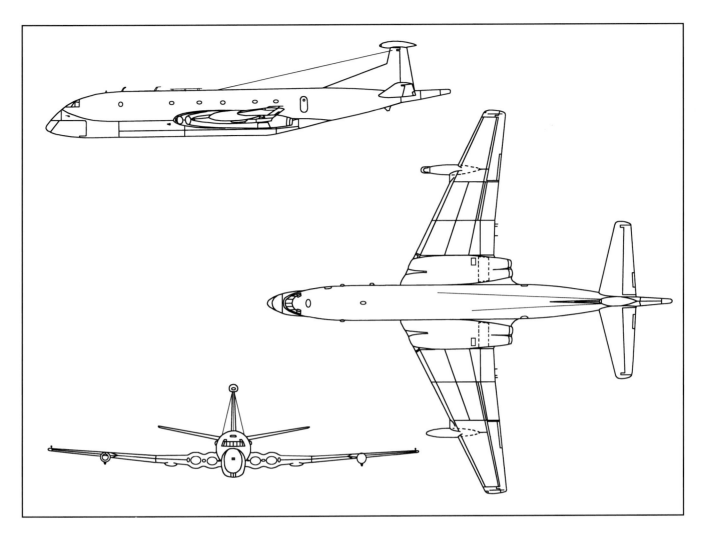

This general arrangement diagram confirms the Comet ancestry that is built into the Nimrod. This is an MR1, the later MR2 features wingtip ESM pods plus a refuelling probe and associated finlet modifications. (BBA Collection)

This view taken almost level with the fintop ESM pod reveals the extensive removable panels built into the Nimrod. Of note are the removed tailplanes to the front of the aircraft. When the AEW fleet was finally written off, as much as possible was recovered. (BBA Collection)

The first manifestation of the Nimrod, the MR1, bore a strong resemblance to the earlier Comet. By the time the MR2 appeared it had gained wingtip ESM pods, an inflight refuelling probe, plus aerodynamic surfaces on the tailplanes and lower fuselage to restore longitudinal stability. (BBA Collection)

As part of the rework process to create the Nimrod, the original Avon engines were replaced by the more powerful R.R. Spey's. Not only does this confer a sprightly performance on the aircraft it has another benefit. This results in the Nimrod being able to cruise on patrol with the outboard engines running at idle thus conserving fuel and extending patrol time. (BBA Collection)

Close to the point of touchdown this Nimrod MR2 shows one of its greatest assets, the 1 million candle power light housed in the front of the wing pinion tank. (BBA Collection)

Taxiing past the photographer this Nimrod MR2 attracts interest from other spectators. A minute later the aircraft collided with a runway sweeper truck which extensively damaged the right-hand wing ESM pod. (BBA Collection)

COMET ALPHABET

2TAF	Second Tactical Air Force		HSA	Hawker Siddeley Aviation
AA	Aerolineas Argentinas		INS	Inertial Navigation System
AAJC	Airline Association Joint Council		IT	Inclusive Tourist
AEW	Airborne Early Warning			
A&AEE	Aircraft & Armament Experimental Establishment		JAL	Japan Air Lines
ADF	Aerial Direction Finder		Lbs.st.	Pounds Static Thrust
AEW	Airborne Early Warning		LORAN	Long Range Air Navigation
AIB	Accident Investigation Board			
ARB	Air(craft) Registration Board			
ASB	Air Safety Board		MA	Malaysian Airways
AREA	Aerovias Ecuatorianas		MAD	Magnetic Anomaly Detector
AUW	All Up Weight		MEA	Middle East Airways
AWACS	Airborne Warning and Control System		MoA	Ministry of Aviation / Aircraft
			MoS	Ministry of Supply
			MOD	Ministry of Defence
BAA	British Airports Authority		MOTU	Maritime Operational Training Unit
BAE Systems	British Aerospace / Systems		MR	Maritime Reconnaissance
BAC	British Aircraft Corporation		MRA	Maritime Reconnaissance Advanced
BEA	British European Airways		MSA	Malaysia Singapore Airways
BLEU	Blind Landing Experimental Unit		MTBF	Mean Time Between Failure
BOAC	British Overseas Airways Corporation			
			OCU	Operational Conversion Unit
BSAA	British South African Airways			
			RAE	Royal Aircraft Establishment
C of A	Certificate of Airworthiness		RAF	Royal Air Force
CAA	Civil Aviation Authority		RCAF	Royal Canadian Air Force
CPA	Canadian Pacific Airways		RN	Royal Navy
			RR	Rolls-Royce
DH	De Havilland			
			SAA	South African Airways
EAA	East African Airways		SAR	Search And Rescue
ECU	Engine Change Unit		SBAC	Society of British Aircraft Constructors
ELINT	Electronic Intelligence (gathering)			
ESM	Electronic Support Measures		TAP	Transportes Aerolineas Portugal
FRS	Fellow of the Royal Society		UAT	Union Aeromaritime de Transport
GFE	Government Furnished Equipment		VIP	Very Important Person
GMT	Greenwich Mean Time			

Still wearing the first Nimrod colour scheme of grey and white is this AEW3 awaiting final disposal at RAF Abingdon. Contrast the revamped front and rear fuselages with the MR version of the same aircraft. (BBA Collection)

Prior to the issuance of disposal instructions this side-on view of a Nimrod AEW3 in store at RAF Abingdon reveals the extensive modifications required to produce this variant. (BBA Collection)

With its front radome removed this Nimrod AEW3 reveals the massive mounting beam required to carry the forward cassegrain scanner. A similar installation was built into the rear fuselage. (BBA Collection)

Although the AEW aircraft were a failure, their disposal and subsequent reduction to parts did have the benefit of increasing the spares inventory for the anti submarine fleet of aircraft. (BBA Collection)

SIGNIFICANT DATES

23 December 1942
Brabazon Committee formed to investigate future of air transport.

9 February 1943
Committee proposals for five basic types of airliner issued in report.

November 1944
De Havilland begins tentative design work.

February 1945
De Havilland issued with instruction to proceed in accordance with Spec S.20/44.

1946
Ministry of Supply issues De Havilland with contract to build two prototypes of a jet-powered airliner later to be named Comet.

1946
BOAC orders 25 of the new airliner although this was later cut to 10.

15 May 1946
First flight of DH108 Swallow tailless swept-wing research aircraft.

21 January 1947
MoS issues ITP for production aircraft.

24 July 1947
First flight of Ghost engine in converted Lancastrian.

27 July 1949
First flight of first Comet prototype.

27 July 1950
First flight of second Comet prototype.

9 January 1951
First production Comet 1 makes maiden flight.

16 February 1952
Development Comet 2X makes first flight.

2 April 1952
First Commercial jet flight in the world made by Comet 1 of BOAC.

11 August 1952
Comet 1A makes maiden flight.

26 October 1952
BOAC Comet 1 crashes on takeoff from Rome.

1953
Pan-Am orders Comet 3.

March 1953
Comet 1 enters RCAF service.

3 March 1953
CPA Comet 1A crashes after takeoff from Karachi.

2 May 1953
BOAC Comet 1 breaks up in midair after departing Karachi.

25 July 1953
BOAC Comet 1 taken off active inventory after landing accident at Karachi.

29 August 1953
Comet 2 production aircraft first flies.

10 January 1954
BOAC Comet 1 breaks up in midair after departing Rome.

11 January 1954
BOAC voluntarily grounds Comet fleet whilst crashes investigated.

23 March 1954
BOAC Comet fleet reinstated.

8 April 1954
BOAC Comet 1 on SAA flight breaks up in midair after departing Rome.

9 May 1954
All commercial Comet 1s world-wide are grounded; C of A withdrawn.

19 July 1954
First flight by sole Comet 3.

7 June 1956
Comet C2 enters RAF service with No. 216 Sqdn.

July 1956
Comet V proposal.

17 April 1957
No. 51 Sqdn RAF receives Comet C2(RC).

27 April 1958
Comet 4 makes maiden flight.

30 September 1958
Comet 4 enters commercial service with BOAC.

4 October 1958
BOAC Comet 4 undertakes first scheduled flight to New York.

27 June 1959
First flight of Comet 4B for BEA.

31 October 1959
First flight of Comet 4C.

1 April 1960
Comet 4B enters regular BEA service.

15 February 1962
No. 216 Sqdn receives Comet C4.

November 1962
Last production Comet 4 completed.

24 November 1965
BOAC retires Comet 4 from service after last commercial flight.

October 1966
Dan Air begins Comet operations.

1967
First flight of Nimrod prototype, a converted Comet.

1 April 1967
Comet C2 retired from RAF service.

October 1969
First Nimrod MR1 enters RAF service with MOTU.

31 October 1973
Last flight of Comet 4 in BEA colours.

1974
No. 51 Sqdn replaces Comets with Nimrod R1.

April 1975
Last Comet C4 retired by No. 216 Sqdn.

23 August 1979
First Nimrod MR2, converted from MR1, re-enters RAF service.

9 November 1980
Dan Air retires last Comet after type's final commercial flight.

14 March 1997
Comet 4 XS235 *Canopus* retired for preservation to Bruntingthorpe.

1999
Conversion programme to produce 21 Nimrod MRA4s from MR2s begins.

2000
Discussions begin amongst interested parties about returning Comet 4 *Canopus* to flying status.

A few Comets survive in preservation. This is C2 XK699 at Lyneham. (BBA Collection)